I0532209

"I recommend this book for anyone who isn't afraid of looking deeper within."
- **Gina Moffa,** LCSW, Psychotherapist and author of *Moving On Doesn't Mean Letting Go*

"*The Truth Teller* takes us through a tale of one's own suffering with easily digested and straight to the point examples of what keeps us "stuck."
- **Dr. Joelle Giacomo,** DSW, LCSW

"...a wonderfully guided tour about listening to your own voice and doing the work to achieve your goals and better understand both your own self and your relationships with others."
- **Eileen M. Schneider,** MSW, LCSW, ACSW

"To unmask, go deeper and understand our true selves and value is something I know I've learned from Emma (and this book) and hope you can too."
- **Eli Weinstein,** LCSW

"The self-proclaimed truth-teller Emma Demar will inspire you to become a truth-seeker."
- **Lexie Manion,** writer, artist, mental health advocate

THE

TRUTH

TELLER

THE TRUTH BEHIND OUR MASKS

EMMA DEMAR, LCSW

A.K.A.
That Trendy Therapist™

THE TRUTH TELLER: The Truth Behind Our Masks

© 2023, Emma Demar. All rights reserved.

Published by That Trendy Therapist Media,
North Bergen, New Jersey

ISBN 979-8-9873332-0-4 (paperback)
ISBN 979-8-9873332-1-1 (eBook)
Library of Congress Control Number: 2023910722

www.thattrendytherapist.com

Without limiting the rights under copyright reserved above, no part of this publication may be reproduced, stored in or introduced into a retrieval system, or transmitted in any form or by any means (electronic, mechanical, photocopying, recording or otherwise whether now or hereafter known), without the prior written permission of both the copyright owner and the above publisher of this book, except by a reviewer who wishes to quote brief passages in connection with a review written for insertion in a magazine, newspaper, broadcast, website, blog or other outlet in conformity with United States and International Fair Use or comparable guidelines to such copyright exceptions.

This book is intended to provide accurate information with regard to its subject matter and reflects the opinion and perspective of the author. However, in times of rapid change, ensuring all information provided is entirely accurate and up-to-date at all times is not always possible. Therefore, the author and publisher accept no responsibility for inaccuracies or omissions and specifically disclaim any liability, loss or risk, personal, professional or otherwise, which may be incurred as a consequence, directly or indirectly, of the use and/or application of any of the contents of this book.

To my Bubbie, whose motto was:

"I am who I am, and I say what I want, and if you don't like it, fuck it."

CONTENTS

PREFACE

"If a truth burns down a relationship, a family, a community, or a society, it was only ever held together by lies. And to that I say, let it burn. I never want to live in a world where our need for 'comfort' supersedes our need to stand on a foundation only the truth can provide."
— Mark Groves (@itsmarkgroves)

O h, hello. I'd like to start by introducing myself and thanking you very much for picking up this book from the shelf (or for clicking "buy now" or whatever it was). Some of you may know me from Instagram or TikTok (I go by @thattrendytherapist). Others may know me personally. Some may even remember me from a little show called "Gossip Girl." (Spotted: the pink minion from season 1 of the original series). And some of you don't know me whatsoever and just picked up this book because, perhaps, it stood out to you in some way. Whatever the reason may be that you found me here, I'm glad that you did.

My name is Emma Demar. I'm a therapist by profession. I say "by profession" because I don't view "therapist" as my entire identity. Being a therapist is an important part of my life, but it's not how I define myself as a person. Furthermore, I've carved out a unique identity for myself *as* a therapist. I am That Trendy Therapist™. I'm a modern and progressive therapist who is up on all the latest societal trends. I love pop culture. I enjoy fashion. I curse in session (my favorite is "fuck"—it comes in handy when you're talking about how much someone has pissed you off). I am an avid user of social media. I'm a therapist who, like I am as a person, will keep it 100% real with you because that's the only way I know how. And because it's what works.

So now that I've introduced myself, let's discuss how this book came to be. Writing was my first love. It's my favorite form of self-expression. I allow the words to pour right from my soul, through my fingertips and onto the keyboard (or through my pen, because sometimes I like to keep it old-school and hand-write. It's a lost art). Writing is an intrinsic need of mine, and as you'll come to know, I'm all about understanding and meeting your intrinsic needs. For as long as I can remember, I've wanted to write a book. I grew up with stacks of short stories on my childhood bookshelves—chapter books that I had written, both fiction and non-fiction, printed out and stapled together with cover art, forewords, and all—isn't that what all ten-year-olds do for fun? I majored in creative writing in college, knowing that writing is a steady art-form of mine that I'd always carry with me and utilize throughout my life. It's how I express myself, make sense of the world, and communicate best to others.

It was during the dead of winter of 2021, whilst still amidst our global pandemic, that I started writing this book. It sort of began to write itself, beginning as journal entries I'd write to process what was currently going on in the world and my feelings about it. Every day, I'd log onto Instagram or open up TikTok to see a plethora of posts about burnout, pandemic fatigue, and seasonal depression. Each day, I'd talk to my clients who were all feeling isolated and disconnected from themselves and the world around them. And of course, like everyone else during lockdown, I felt trapped and stifled. As a creative, I needed an outlet to channel all my pent-up pandemic feelings into some form of art. I found it through writing and social media.

Alongside my journaling, I started posting insightful, confrontive, and hard-hitting quotes I found that spilled truth with no apologies. I originally viewed my account as simply a creative outlet where I could share my innermost thoughts and ideas with others. I posted quotes that resonated with me and that I intuitively felt my followers would see themselves in and that would strike a chord in a meaningful way. In the captions, I'd let my creative writing and psychology backgrounds collide as I expanded on the concept of the topic of the quote. As my account steadily grew, it became clear that these posts resonated deeply with my followers. My page was no longer just a creative outlet for me, but a home base where others could find inspiration and feel seen. I've always felt tuned into the collective consciousness and have an innate ability to translate these concepts through words. Soon after I started posting the quotes with my lengthy captions, I started getting messages from my followers saying that I'd made them think about things in a way they hadn't before or thanking me for putting into words what they'd been struggling to express themselves. One thing I've gathered over the course of three years of my daily posts is that my words make people feel seen, understood, and more connected to themselves and others. And if they can do that, then by all means, I'm here for it! So, I turned my daily insights into a whole ass book.

This book is my truth. It's about how I found my inner truth and learned to stand by it no matter what. We all have our own inner truths. These truths whisper in our ears to remind us of how we really feel about something, deep down.

We cannot ignore these truths because they impact us in a profound way, even if we do our best to avoid paying them any attention. And especially then. Because if we don't decide, consciously, to recognize and bring them to light, they will rule us without us having any say in the matter. Our inner truth is the voice of our own inner child. It's the voice we know without words. We all have these deep-seated truths, but some of these truths are buried so deep that we cannot even locate them anymore. And what's your truth worth if you can't identify it? If you can't identify it, you can't stick by it. And if you can't stick by it, you're at risk of feeling empty inside. You're at risk of feeling unfulfilled. If you don't know who you are, you will always feel like a piece is missing. You will be in danger of following the flow of others instead of your own. You will risk waking up one day realizing you have a hole inside that you don't know how to fill. So, fill it now or regret it later. The choice, of course, is yours.

If you choose to come along this journey of self-discovery, you're a courageous one. Allow this book to be your personal roadmap on your journey to discover your inner truth teller. This book will encourage you to dig deep and confront yourself. I'm going to ask probing questions that will make you think and feel that which has, perhaps, been suppressed or long forgotten. And I hope you have the guts to stick with the parts that might challenge you or make you uncomfortable. Growth is uncomfortable. But you'll never regret it. I want to help you take a closer look at those grey areas inside of you that need clarity. We all have a story and a truth to reflect on, but we don't always do the reflecting. We all have a voice, but we don't always use it. In our society, we are confronted with a lot of opinions and suggestions and commands about who we "should" be or what our life "should" look like, and often that overwhelming feedback paralyzes us and makes us lose sight of ourselves. The closer you are to your inner truth, the more self-assured you will become. The more self-assured you are, the more confident you'll feel about yourself and the choices you make every day. The more aligned you'll be. The safer you'll feel in the world. The more at peace you'll be. And don't we all want to feel at peace?

As I guide you towards your inner truth, I'm going to share bits and pieces of my own journey. I'll share my story a few different ways. First, I'll use personal anecdotes throughout the chapters. Second, you'll find poems between each chapter that I've written throughout my life. These poems and anecdotes are used to illustrate my points. Also, I feel that sharing our personal stories is what connects us. Perhaps some of my own experiences will resonate with you, or maybe yours will look entirely different. That's okay. Feel free to disregard anything that doesn't fit. After all, there is no "right way" to do the inner work. I can't promise you that everything I share will resonate or apply to your particular situation, but I can promise that I will tell my truth and provide you with my insights from what I've learned. And hopefully, those insights will help you in some way on your own journey.

This book is about coming back to you. It's an opportunity to take a deep dive into your psyche and locate both the wounds and treasures that make you who you are. This is a safe space. You will be confronted, yes, but with great care. Read this book by yourself and allow it to take you on whatever journey it does, naturally. There are no rules. Allow whatever it is that comes up to surface and move through you. This is how the inner work is done. Remember, I'm here to help you find that truth within yourself. The truth about your story. The truth about how you look at the world. *The truth about you.* My hope is that, in reading this book, you become more in tune with who you are at your core. And, even more than that, that you'll find the courage to live as your authentic self and express this authenticity in your daily life. This book is your guide to becoming your own truth teller.

As a person, I am fully true to who I am. I will say what is in my heart. I live by what is in my soul. I wrote this book to share the power of living in your authentic truth with as many of you as I can. I know what it's like to live not embodying your full self, and it's something I would never go back to. The truth is that a lot of us are sleepwalking through our lives. We're living life on the sidelines like spectators. We're not fully awake, or fully present, to the here and now. We aren't tuned in. We go about our lives haphazardly disconnected from our true selves and our inner knowing. We've convinced ourselves that we're "right" about our viewpoints and few of us are truly open to changing them. We are out of touch with our humanity. And our society, that is engineered on social media and face-tuned to the tenth degree, is bogged down with so much unnecessary shit that it's suffocating. And paralyzing. We need to begin to locate ourselves as individuals so that we can better locate one another.

We need more active listening and less listening to react. We need more understanding. We need less small-talk and deeper connections. We *want* to feel more connected. We *long* for it. It's a fundamental need. And it's a fundamental need that we, as a culture, are not addressing. We need less black-and-white thinking and more nuance. Only our own truths should be left defined and in bold. We need to know our truth. Our truth is our starting point. It's how we orient ourselves within the world. It's the lens through which we interpret things, which is unique to ourselves and the product of our upbringing, our society, and our innate nature. We need this understanding to guide us as individuals, so that we can come together collectively from healed and conscious places. It starts with the individual.

But in our society, we often overlook the individual. We focus on the group. We view it as selfish to take time out of our day to think about ourselves. We do self-care, but then we feel guilty about it. We don't say how we feel because we don't want to rock the boat. We don't think our opinion really matters. So, we routinely suppress our inner truth. And in suppressing our inner selves, we lose our ability to connect deeply with ourselves and one another. We're looking in each other's eyes but we're not really seeing what's there. How can you possibly see what is there when you can't see that very thing within yourself? We can only form connections that are as deep as the connection we have with ourselves. We need the courage to go deeper. We need more people willing to let their masks down and be honest. We need more authenticity. We need more sincerity. We need more truth.

But people are living by mottos like "go with the flow" and "kindness is cool"—which is great and all, but also can be very unhealthy when applied loosely to everything. Some things are better handled with realness. Some things require intention. Sometimes people are being *performatively* nice, which isn't genuine. And we don't like to look at that part. We overlook the actual intentions behind our words and actions. Because looking at our deeper motivations forces us to look at our shadow. The shadow is our dark part. We all have one, and it's essential to get to know it because whether or not we want to face it, it plays an essential role in who we are. Some of us are tapped into it and some run from it as fast as they fucking can. And guess what? They never stop running. They sprint through their lives and they're never in the same place long enough to reap the immense benefits of any experience. We desperately need to begin to embody our inner truths and to become our own truth tellers. So, what's the key? It's called tuning in. And you have to tune out to tune in.

I long for the expanse
An enormous exhale that envelopes
The entirety of space
The stampede of noise here
Is deafening
It tramples upon my eardrums
Shrieking its nonsense
Tossing noise that's hollow
But way out there, I can hear
The thoughts that have been
Trampled on
The intricate web of feelings
Cluttered by those of others
The convoluted knot of confusion
That's not my own
Out there, I have a knowing
A deep well of truth that's brewing
It's too vast to be released here
To fall on deaf ears
The animals, the plants, the rugged
Terrain, it needs nothing from me
It didn't ask, like everything here
Belting out needs and bumping
Into one another with abandon
Lacking clarity
Out there, they know the truth
They're still, so they can hear it
They are it without pretending
My soul swells with the yearning
Until I can breathe again.

The Truth Teller, written in the summer of 2021 before my trip to Kenya

CHAPTER 1

THE TRUTH ABOUT
NOISE

"Of all the varieties of modern pollution,
noise is the most insidious."
— *Robert Lacey*

We can't get to our inner truth while being bombarded by external noise—and we live in a world full of noise. I'm not just talking about the sound of car horns or crying babies or your neighbor who plays their music obnoxiously loud until all hours of the night. Of course, there's all that noise. But the noise I'm referring to, here, is anything outside of yourself that can serve as a distraction from your *own* voice. Each day there are countless noises vying for your attention. It's far easier to get swept up in the noise than it is to find ways to tune it out and come back to you.

Now, before I go further, let me address something some of you may be thinking. Why would you want to tune into your inner voice? Why not just keep things light? Let's keep life simple, right guys? There are many people who think this way, and you may be one of them. And it's important to look closely into why that is. Why are you uncomfortable at the very thought of going deeper (with yourself or others)? What are you avoiding by keeping things surfacy? Are you really getting all that you can out of life, or a relationship, or situation, if you're not putting your whole self into it? Of course not. So, maybe, consider broadening your perspective on this. Perhaps you could really benefit from tuning into yourself and becoming more self-aware.

Also, many people decide prematurely whether something is or isn't for them. We tend to think that our way is the "right" way. But what if that's just fear talking? Consider that your avoidance of delving deeper and questioning your ingrained patterns is taking the easy way out. Not tuning in is actually the safe way out. It's very simple to never do the self-inquiry or reflect on anything in your life. This kind of work ain't easy, that's for sure! And that's why many people avoid it altogether. Confronting yourself takes strength and courage. The silence of your own thoughts and feelings can be frightening if you've spent your life trying to dull down your inner voice. So here I challenge you: it's time to turn down the volume on that external noise so that all you have left to focus on is what's within. This is where the inner work begins.

I've always valued silence. Because, in the silence, I can find my truth. Silence is where I come back to myself. I can't hear myself think when I'm surrounded by a group of people trying to talk over one another, and honestly, neither can you. Whether you're an extrovert or introvert, you won't be able to hear your inner truth speaking to you if you're constantly surrounded by external noise. You can get your energy from a crowded room, sure, but you're not going to be able to tune into what your inner voice is whispering to you if you have your friend over there gabbing their opinion over the music, are you?

Any pivotal change or epiphany I've had in my life has come from a place of silence. When I'm able to tune out all the distractions and listen to what my soul is telling me, everything becomes clearer. In my recovery from my eating disorder (we'll get to this), I spent a lot of time by myself. This was a choice I made with intent because I knew it was necessary in order for me to have any sort of lasting growth. Anyone could tell me to recover or to eat. But I knew I wasn't going to actually stick to any form of recovery unless I'd chosen it myself. And that goes with any change. If you're not choosing the change for yourself, because you know it's what's best for you, chances are you're not going to stick with it. Why? Because it doesn't come from your inner truth, and therefore, you don't have the personal motivation for it. You'll never stick with something in the long run if you don't have that personal investment. There's no voice more powerful than that of your inner truth teller.

Perhaps the sweetest sense of silence I've ever experienced was on a family trip to Kenya in the summer of 2021. It was a trip that had been postponed from 2020, and by the time COVID allowed us to go, I was itching for the quiet. There's always noise, but perhaps never more so than during the global pandemic. You couldn't go outside without hearing someone's political views or thoughts on vaccinations. You couldn't turn on the television without an onslaught of opinions and projections and developing news stories. If you weren't grounded during that time, you were going to be easily swept away in the ruckus of noise and distraction. And many of us were. In fact, I'd venture to say that many of us are *still* lost, trying to locate our own truth after several years of hearing those with contradictory opinions screaming over one another. Collectively, we're feeling disoriented and off balance. That's what will happen after a collective trauma. And the pandemic *was* a collective trauma—FYI—and that's not something we can just brush under the rug. Nor should we.

So, I was longing for the vast escape of silence that I knew awaited me in Africa. More than that, I couldn't wait to get back to the basics. We live in an ever-changing, fast-paced society where we glorify being busy and staying on the grind. *Simultaneously, we undervalue the importance of sitting with ourselves and our feelings.* And this is one reason so many people freaked out when they were forced to sit inside with themselves during the pandemic. They may have never done it before, and many didn't know how. Especially those who'd never been in therapy or who'd previously spent their entire existence running from one thing to the next.

Fortunately, as a therapist and someone who makes self-work a daily practice, I wasn't faced with a shock to my emotional system when the quarantine blues set in. But I still turned inward, as I always do when times get tough. I turned to my creativity to express myself. I did a lot of journaling. I dove deep into my yoga practice. I read books on the Enneagram, a personality typing system, that I now incorporate into my work with my patients. I started to write this book. (It is with a *great* deal of gratitude that I did not personally experience any major loss during the pandemic, and my heart goes out to those who did. Moreover, I know that a trip to Kenya was a *massive* privilege, for which I'm entirely grateful). Without the excess noise and distractions of the world, I was able to focus on what it was my soul was pulling me toward and what I was really meant to do with my time. I found my flow.

In Africa, I was met with utter peace and sweet silence. The vast landscapes of rolling terrain and animals traipsing through in their natural habitat engulfed me in a warmth of knowing. *This is what life is about.* It's the natural rhythm of the land, of nature, that we forget about when we are lost in the grind of our artificially-induced society. The animals know intrinsically what they're meant to do. They know how to spot predators, how to find food, when to sleep and how to play.

They don't need an alarm clock. They don't need a weather app to tell them when the rain is coming. Why? *Because they follow their instincts.* They're tuned into their instincts because it's all they have, and, truthfully, all they need. They're able to survive in the wilderness because they know how. And we know how, too, if we allow ourselves. Why wouldn't we allow ourselves to survive on our instincts? Because we don't trust them. Because society likes to present us with conflicting opinions about the "right" way to be. And the more that we make a conscious effort to tune out the noise and tune into ourselves, the better we'll be able to figure out what belongs to us and what doesn't. In other words, we'll be able to identify ourselves more clearly and figure out what applies to us and what we can disregard. We'll know what we personally think, feel and need. And when we can identify our personal needs and desires, we have an opportunity to meet them.

See, there's a difference between being selfish and doing the self-work. The two get confused often, so let's distinguish one from the other. Being selfish is *only* caring about yourself. A selfish person is someone who lacks consideration for others and only does things for their own personal benefit. But doing the self-work doesn't mean that you don't care about others. It just means you *also* care about yourself, and that you put yourself first because you know that you can't give to others from a true place of generosity and abundance if you're pouring from an empty cup. The self-work is something that we, as human beings, all require and deserve. We need to have a certain level of self-awareness so that we can bring our own unique strengths to the world and allow our voices to be heard. We need to have the information to know how to cope with our triggers. We need to have the language to understand our feelings and to express them. Without this self-inquiry, you're missing vital information about yourself. Your roadmap is missing essential pieces. And perhaps, that's why you're feeling lost.

Tuning into yourself doesn't mean you're tuning other people out completely. It doesn't mean that you don't care about, respect, or value the opinions of others. It just means that you respect your own. It means that you see the inherent value within yourself. It means you have your own beliefs that you stand by. It doesn't mean those beliefs can't change and evolve as you grow. They can and they will. But when you're not tuned in, there's a certain level of disconnection that exists between yourself and others. Tuning into yourself will help you more effectively tune into those around you and to our world at large.

The more that you understand and accept your own complexities, the better you'll be able to understand (and tolerate) the complexities of others.

Maybe you're someone who gets bothered a lot. You're bothered by the way people speak or how they deal with things. You're always feeling frustrated. You don't understand why people are acting in this way or that way. But maybe you'd have a better understanding and tolerance for other people, in general, if you were more aware and accepting of your *own* inner complexities. We all have them. And you don't know what lives inside of you unless you face it. Maybe you don't have to be so bothered. Maybe you don't need that chip on your shoulder. Maybe, the more that you can show yourself grace and compassion, the more able (and willing) you'll be to give that back to others. In fact, the next time someone pisses you off, tuning in might be your best move.

Now, I'm not saying you need to spend your days staring at a blank wall in order to find your quiet. I'm also not saying you need to book a trip to Kenya to tune in. Find what works for you. Take a hike—literally. Breathe in the fresh air and don't bring your phone with you. Look up and look out and take in your surroundings. You don't need music. Nature will provide you with music if you allow yourself to hear it. Observe what's around you, without judgment. Or go to a museum. Take your time staring at the artwork. Stay for as long as you like. This is about finding your *own* flow, after all. Take a bath. Take a walk on the beach. Whatever you choose to do, don't bring along any extra noise with you. The point is to be able to hear your intuition speak, which you simply can't do when you're bombarded with external demands of any sort.

You also can't hear your inner truth if you're always talking. Oftentimes, it's the very people who fill the space with their external voice that are most disconnected from their voice within. They love to hear themselves talk, yes, but many are coming from a place of fear. They're *afraid* to take in new information, and frankly they aren't open to it. They don't *want* to listen because listening might mean their ideas and opinions will be threatened somehow. And often, when you're out of touch with your internal truth, you cling onto external systems to help guide you. People who don't trust their inner knowing don't want their life mottos to be questioned because their mottos are all they have. But you can't grow without being challenged. You can't evolve as a human being if you're not taking in new information. Less talking, more listening.

The truth about the noise is that you will get lost in it if you aren't highly attuned to your *own* voice. That's why many people spend their entire existence bouncing from one noise to the next. They don't *want* to hear themselves think because it's too painful and frightening to sit alone with your thoughts if you're not used to it. And I understand that. But you have to begin somewhere. It's part of the work, and no one said the work was easy. It's much easier to distract your way through a moment or a feeling than it is to sit with it. But in the long run, when life does force you to slow down (which it will, inevitably, just like it did during the pandemic), those who don't know how to sit in silence are the ones who will feel depressed, lost, and empty. Those who find their inner truth have a compass to guide them through life. *You have to tune out to tune in.* If you're interested in growth while feeling consistently grounded, you'll need to get quiet and connect to the part of yourself that you've been ignoring: your inner truth.

From where she stood
Beneath the trees of evergreen
Watching the clouds scurry
Past themselves as they played
Hide and seek, she pondered
How long it would take to
Feel as free as the sky seemed
She searched amongst the branches
For short cuts that she could use
As secret steppingstones
To bring her closer to the light
If only she could find out before twilight
What the birds whispered to one another
As they traced patterns along the skyline
But with all her focus upward
She couldn't see the crumbling
Concrete beneath her feet
That swallowed her untied
Shoelaces whole
Just like her soul.

The Truth Teller

CHAPTER 2

THE TRUTH ABOUT
GROUNDING

"Flying starts from the ground. The more grounded you are, the higher you fly."
— J. R. Rim

Everyone is too busy focusing on how to elevate to realize they have no ground to build upon. As a culture, we've glorified the hustle and the desire to achieve as much as humanly possible in this lifetime. It's always about the next thing or running away from the past thing. And, sadly, many of us don't pay attention to the personal cost of the grind. There's an enormous blind spot when it comes to our societal obsession with leveling up. And the blind spot is that you can't possibly ascend if you have not yet mastered grounding. In other words, you can't expect to flourish in life if your roots aren't established, first.

My dad, a highly visual and creative man, once explained to me an analogy that he uses in his life to guide him. My dad is a very grounded individual. He's our family's rock. This analogy is something I continually use to help me conceptualize my life and remind me of the natural order of growth. He described life as building a house. In order to build your house and eventually get to constructing and decorating all of the lavish rooms at the top, you have to start with a solid foundation. You can't create the top part without something to build on, otherwise it will all come crashing down. This is one of the many reasons why you see so many short-lived careers and childhood celebrities who fall from grace. They've pushed and pushed to make it to the top, but they're on a shaky or non-existent foundation. Why? Because they haven't taken the *time* to build a solid foundation for whatever the reason (intentionally or not), and perhaps they never learned the *value* of having a solid base from which to build. Yes, it takes a lot of effort to create that foundation, and it happens over time.

But you can't build anything without something to build upon.

Grounding is laying the building blocks of your truth and what your life is going to be about. The foundation contains your values and your purpose. For example, my foundation includes my values of living authentically; respecting myself first and foremost; choosing quality over quantity in all things; embracing family and good friends; taking care of my health; knowing my worth; speaking my truth; and inspiring and helping others to connect to *their* inner truths. If these core values weren't part of my foundation, then I would be acting from a place of emptiness. I'd go after my dreams without a clear understanding of *why* I'm pursuing these dreams. Or, perhaps, I wouldn't even go after my dreams because I hadn't taken the time to build the fundamentals. We love shortcuts and ways to cheat the system, but anytime someone does that it catches up with them. We all know those people.

In our world today, we have many copycat and performative careers. We have people who are pursuing paths, such as influencers on social media, simply because others have glamorized a lifestyle. Or because people view certain careers as status symbols or a path to celebrity. Or because their parents have pressured them to pursue whatever profession they want them to. They're not always pursuing these paths out of pure passion. And then they get burned out and wonder why. You burn out when you're not connected to your purpose; or to your "why." If you don't know *why* it is you're doing what you're doing, and if it's not coming from a conscious place in your soul, you're not going to feel empowered by it. You'll always feel like you're working for some external source that has no real value to you as an individual. There's a difference between working from a place of passion and working from a place of obligation. There's a difference between pursuing a passion because you feel it's your calling and pursuing one because you're craving external validation. Each of these looks and feels vastly different. (And, yes, I do realize it's a privilege to work from a place of passion. But there is also truth in *finding* and *creating* your why, even when you're in a career that wasn't entirely your choice.)

This is precisely why I could never do a typical desk job. I grew up with a boss of mother who is a C-suite executive and the epitome of a badass woman at the top of the corporate ladder. She makes it look easy when I know it's anything but, and I admire her greatly for how she carries herself as a female leader in business. She grew up without a lot of resources and worked her way up because she decided to. She highly values independence, and she didn't want to ever have to rely on anyone. This has worked for her because it's her purpose. She has worked her way up continually because she's connected to a purpose that she finds personal value in. If she didn't have that foundation of truth to propel herself forward, I'm not sure how she could have stuck it out with as much vigor as she does, day after day, year after year. It's highly impressive, to say the least.

But, for me, I always knew I would not be a corporate gal. And, luckily, neither of my parents ever pressured me or even slightly suggested that I follow their paths. Even though I'm a creative, like my product designer dad, neither my mother nor father ever assumed I'd want to follow their career paths. Because of this, and because I know I'm the type of person who needs passion to fuel me day in and day out, I was able to take the time to figure out what I wanted to do from the ground up. As a creative, I'm inspired by different routines each day. I'm energized by the ability to create that which makes people feel something, like a podcast episode or one of my daily Instagram posts. It's what keeps me going and gets me out of bed each morning. I find meaning in creating and self-expression. That's my truth. It's part of my foundation. I knew that—as someone who values authenticity—I would never be happy or fulfilled in a job that I felt no personal connection with. I needed to build from within and to create a career that stemmed from my *own* values and identity. I knew intuitively that if I didn't build from that base, I wouldn't stick with it. Why? Because it wouldn't feel authentic to me, and thus it wouldn't feel fulfilling or worthwhile. And if it doesn't feel fulfilling or worthwhile, you're not going to be putting your best self forward.

But my journey here wasn't without its own trials, tribulations, and deep moments of reflection. First, I had to figure out my foundation. Like I said, we live in a society that glamorizes the grind. So, after college, I figured the next obvious step would be to get myself a corporate gig in the city. I found myself doing a few month-long internships and stints at different office jobs such as working in HR at a bank, as an advertising creative, a feature editor at a luxury travel magazine, and more. None of these jobs lasted long because my heart wasn't in it. I was there because I thought I had to be. I thought, like many of us do, that my only option was to do what society expected of me: to get a 9:00-5:00 job that was in line with my degree. I had a Bachelor's Degree in creative writing, so I assumed the obvious next step would be to find a career that utilized my writing skills, that was salary-based, and looked good on a résumé.

The truth was that I hated every second of those jobs. I felt like I was putting on a costume every day when I put on my blazer and work dresses and clutched my mom's hand-me-down designer briefcase. It wasn't me—and I knew that. I knew I wasn't going to be able to spend my entire life feeling like it was Halloween every time I went to work (which is most days of many of our lives if we're being honest). So, I began to think outside the box. I tuned out the outside noise, and I sat and thought about my next steps. Because, of course, any important decision in my life has originated in a moment of silence. I *could've* polled my family and friends to see what *they* thought I should do with my career, but I knew they had their own biases and didn't know any better than I did what path was meant for me. What was I going to do with my life that felt meaningful to *me*? I'd decided to start there and create a career around whatever that was.

One evening, as I sat in my childhood bedroom staring out the window contemplating life (one of my favorite past times), the idea came. This was my intuition speaking to me. And because I was sitting in silence and listening for it, I was able to hear it. I had tuned out to tune in. I was going to use what I'd learned through my recovery from my eating disorder to be a therapist who specializes in eating disorders. I was going to make meaning out of the fact that I went through such an intense trauma in my life and made it out on the other side. I'd use all that I learned to help others find their own light. I've always loved helping people. I was always that friend others came to for advice. And I loved having deep talks more than anything else. So why not do that? I could make my own schedule, feel inspired every day using my own experiences to help those around me, and have time for my own creativity as well. And that's exactly what I did.

I went to Fordham University for my Masters in Social Work and started a two-year fellowship immediately upon graduating, at a private practice called Intrinpsych Woman where I knew I could see myself working after the fellowship ended. I've been there ever since. I got my hours toward my full licensure, passed my Licensed Clinical Social Worker (LCSW) exam, and am now a licensed clinician in the state of New York. I'm a partner, with my amazing business partner and former supervisor, Camilla Mager, at the private practice where I started as a fellow. Camilla has been an immense source of knowledge, support and guidance in my work thus far as a therapist. I work with individuals struggling with eating disorders, body image, confidence, anxiety, and many other related presenting problems. I am a supervisor to a therapist who is getting *her* hours toward licensure. And, I have time for my own creativity. I've built up my own trademarked brand—That Trendy Therapist™—on social media and have written for various mental health websites as a freelance writer. I collaborate frequently with other mental health professionals on podcasts, Instagram lives, webinars, and more. Every day, I do something creative. Every day, I try to inspire others. Every day, I feel like myself. I don't compromise myself. I don't sell my soul. I create and work directly from my soul. And I get paid for it!

Because I took the time to build my foundation before beginning my career, I never have a moment where I'm questioning if it's really for me. I know it is because I've chosen it consciously. Everything about what I stand for as a person is reflected in my career. My personal values are aligned with my job. Of course, as a human being, I have days where I feel less motivated than others, but it's never because I'm not fully invested in what I'm doing. It's always easy for me to jump back into things when the motivation returns because I have that grounding and I find enormous meaning in what I do. That's the benefit of having a solid foundation.

Now, let's get this out of the way, because I have a strong hunch what some of you are thinking. As I've said before, I *know* what a privilege it is to be able to make a conscious choice about what you want to do with your life. Not everyone has that opportunity or ability, whether for financial reasons, family obligations, or other restrictions or limitations. But that doesn't mean that you can't build a foundation. It doesn't change the fact that you can and should still find your "why." And finding your "why" doesn't only pertain to your career. It can also be what you do in your spare time. Let's say you're a part-time student and have a plethora of loans to pay off, so you're working several part-time jobs on the side. It may feel impossible to feel any sense of connection to what you're doing because it's not at all where you want to be. But challenge yourself to see if you can find some sense of meaning or purpose. Maybe there's one small aspect of your job that energizes you, or there's a fellow employee who makes you smile. Or maybe you can feel some sense of joy about what you're studying in school and the doors it might open for you in the future. Or maybe you've been someone who has historically struggled to keep *any* job, and the fact that you're holding one down at all is an accomplishment in and of itself. Perhaps you can find your purpose in your hobby and allow that passion to exist on the side of what you do for money. Find the meaning. That is your foundation. That is your why.

The truth is that the way that we design our life is a mirror of what's within us. The risks you take in life are generally proportionate to how safe you feel in the world and how much you trust yourself. If you're keeping your life routine, well, that tells you something. There's nothing wrong with routine in and of itself. But what's your relationship to your routine? Do you rely on it to the extent that any changes to this routine cause you to spiral and feel out of control? Are you able to be flexible when need be? Perhaps keeping your life routine and predictable is a result of you being afraid. And it's important to understand where this fear is coming from. There's not much growth or joy in keeping things safe. If you're only using one route on your road map, you'll never reap the immense benefits of what can be found on alternative routes. You get to create your life. And the point is to create it with intention. Because however you design it will have an enormous impact on your mental health.

Take a closer look at your foundation. Ask yourself how sturdy you feel. How supported do your feet feel on the ground? Why is it difficult for you to ground yourself in situations that feel unfamiliar? What comes up? You can always come back to your foundation, and you should from time to time. Make sure it's truly working for you and assisting in your growth, not holding you back from opportunities that would expand your consciousness and assist in your self-development. Question if your foundation is holding you back or enabling you to move forward and adapt to all that life throws your way. And if it's not working for you, there's always the opportunity to re-evaluate and make the necessary adjustments.

GROUNDING

Wherever you come from, and whatever opportunities you may or may not have, you can create a foundation. This foundation will consist of your personal values and what you want your life to mean. Think about looking back on your life and how you'll feel about the path you chose. Visualize it and sit with the feelings that arise. Stop talking to this person and that person about what you should or shouldn't be doing. They all have their own agenda and honestly, the more opinions you're bombarded with, the more confused you'll be. Remember, we're trying to *lessen* the unnecessary noise, not add more of it. Allow yourself the opportunity to get in touch with what your inner truth is saying to you. This goes for anything—career, hobbies, relationships, making any sort of life decision—all these things should stem from your foundation. And if you're interested in ascending and having a life that you can be genuinely proud of, it's going to start with laying down the groundwork for yourself. You simply can't build the future you desire if you're not grounded in your truth.

We are collectively stifled
Gasping for air behind pieces
Of fabric clutching our face
Under which we swallow back
The truths we long to scream
And we say we don't know why
Even though it's blindingly clear
As we toss one mask out
Just to slap on another
Not bothering to breathe
In between or to feel seen
Because, behind here, we can hide

Yet still, we don't know why
We feel suffocated and invisible
We are clones of one another
Stuffing our truths behind
Our uniforms in this school of lies
And we all don't feel alive
And, somehow, we don't know why.

The Truth Teller, written in late 2021 during the pandemic

CHAPTER 3

THE TRUTH ABOUT
UNMASKING

"Do they love you or the mask you put on every day?"
— Shimika Bowers

ow that we've tuned out the noise and discussed the importance of our foundation, let's talk about what's blocking us from accessing our truth. You read the title: we're talking about our masks. I know many of us now viscerally cringe when we read or hear the word "masks." I, for one, certainly do. So, let's ground ourselves in the truth that, of course, "masks" can trigger us with their obvious connotation (we just went through a global pandemic clothed in masks, hello). But we need to talk about *another* form of masks we commonly wear: our figurative masks. You know, the ones we wear in public (or even in private) that serve as a protective barrier or a shield we can hide behind? Yeah, those. Because our figurative masks, which many of us don't even realize we're wearing, prevent us from getting to know ourselves and one another on a deeper level.

We adopt these figurative masks subconsciously as a means of survival. Sometimes, something that happened to us in our past made us feel like we needed to dull down or hide certain parts of ourselves. Or, because of past trauma, we feel the need to adopt a persona to send out into the world instead of our true selves because it feels safer that way. This persona has the characteristics that you don't. Maybe you feel broken and weak inside, so you adopt a tough exterior in order to get by. Or perhaps you've been told you're "too much" so you adopt the mask of being pleasant and appeasing at all times. The figurative mask is adopted as a means of self-protection, and it often occurs at a subconscious level (hence why you may be unaware that you're even wearing it). But the issue with these masks is that you're sending a false or a limited identity out into the world that doesn't accurately align with your inner truth. And not only can this mask get in the way of you forming healthy relationships with others, but it'll prevent you from attending to your deeper wounds within.

Let's take a look behind some of these masks we commonly see in our society. One of these may resonate with you, and if so, use it to take a deeper look behind the metaphorical fabric. One kind of mask is the "I'm a perfect person" mask. This person is the perfectionist. They strive to be the perfect example in all ways, always. They aim to never make a mistake, and they're extremely tough on themselves if they do. They're highly critical of both themselves and others, always trying to correct and perfect. What's behind this mask? Perhaps this individual grew up with a parent or caregiver that was very critical of them, and they began to internalize this inner critic. They learned to self-correct their behavior before anyone else could correct them from the outside. It feels safer and less of a threat that way. This mask makes it *seem* as though the perfectionist has it all under control, but underneath they're incredibly anxiety-ridden and are constantly trying to reach the feeling of "just right." As much as they try and correct themselves, those around them, and their environment, they never truly feel that things are all right, just as they're meant to be. Because, reality is, there's no such thing as perfection. They'll always be searching for it.

Another kind of mask we commonly see is the "I'm here to help!" mask. This mask is worn by the people-pleaser who grew up feeling like they didn't receive the same love and attention everyone else got. Consequently, they adopted the internal belief that they're not intrinsically worthy of love. So, in order to acquire that love and to feel deserving of it, they learned to do things for others so that they could "earn" this love. The mask covers up the underlying motivation behind the "giving nature" of the people-pleaser. The truth is that they're not just giving from the goodness of their hearts. They're pouring from an empty cup. They're giving to get. It's transactional. Their "good deeds" come with unwritten expectations. But the more they give, the more they feel taken advantage of. They, unknowingly, teach others to love them not for who they are (as they truly desire) but for what they do for them. They end up resentful and never feel that they're enough.

Then there's the "I come in peace" mask. This mask is worn by the peacekeeper. This person is always seemingly "zen" and they strive to keep the peace at all costs. They're often those who've experienced something early on in their life that made them feel unbalanced, like a loss or a sudden change of environment, and they're longing for stability. They want to feel external and internal peace and to have those both in harmony with one another. This individual often fears disconnection from others, but what they don't realize is that they only become *more* disconnected in their quest for that peace. Because in order to feel peaceful all of the time, one has to zone out to life and avoid the natural highs and lows that come along with it. The truth about the peacekeeper is that they crave this sense of peace not simply because they're "zen" by nature, but because they're terrified of being destabilized. Their inner truth is that they're not actually as peaceful as they present themselves to be. They're simply detached. They routinely ignore and avoid the issues in their life that desperately need to be addressed until it's too late. And then an explosion erupts. And then their environment is truly off-balance.

Then we've got the "I'm a good guy" mask. This mask is worn by the person who has a deep need for people to see them as "good." They might have grown up with a parent who was unpredictable in some way, or a parent who served more as a peer than as a protector, and they thus developed a conflicting relationship with authority. They don't trust authority, but more so than that, they don't trust their *inner* sense of authority. That is, they don't trust *themselves*. They rely on a trusted group of alliances to make them feel safe and whom they know they can go to for guidance. The "good guy" puts up a pleasant exterior, but this is used as a defense mechanism so that they won't feel attacked. They deeply fear being blamed and have a difficult time tolerating their own discrepancies. They project their fears onto others. And, in doing so, they unknowingly create distance in their relationships with their constant questioning of others' intentions. People may know them as a "good person" who goes with the flow of life, but what they're avoiding is their *own* flow. Perhaps they're not always coming from a place of genuine kindness, but from a deep-seated fear of not having support because they don't feel safe in the world.

Whatever your figurative mask may be, it's essential to understand what it is and why you've been wearing it. We need to learn the story behind our masks so that we can adequately address our fundamental, underlying needs that aren't being attended to. What mask are you wearing? How did you adopt this particular mask? Where did you pick it up along the way?

Has it served you well? In what ways has it held you back? Your mask isn't your fault. Shaming yourself isn't going to do you any good. It's about developing awareness and understanding. It's about recognizing that your figurative mask *isn't* your true nature. It's an adapted version of you that you've developed as a response to events that happened to you in your upbringing. There's a *reason* that you adopted your figurative mask. And while it may have protected you in certain ways along your journey, you cannot grow or evolve into your highest self if you continue to wear it.

Taking off your figurative mask will feel very scary, and that's just the truth. Because taking it off requires you to show up to your life as yourself, authentically. Taking it off requires you to be truthful and transparent with yourself and others. To live without a mask on is to stand tall in your naked truth and not apologize for it. It's being able to meet your own reflection without immediately running away. It's about being able to sit with yourself and others—*not* just when things are peaceful and light-hearted, but when times are tough and sticky and dark. There's a vulnerability in revealing our full selves to the world and meeting the eyes of others while embodying that full self. Most of us are never brave enough to do it. But this is the work that needs to be done to get to know who it is you are at your core.

We wear masks to protect ourselves. No one wants to feel vulnerable and exposed. But as we know, true strength lives in vulnerability. When we wear our masks, no one can see our truth. And if we wear them long enough, we start to fool ourselves into believing we can keep them on and operate like this forever. But then, gradually, we lose our grasp on our own identity. We become clones so that we can feel the safety of belonging and blending in, all while stuffing down that which makes us unique. In turn, we quiet our inner voice that internally whispers our truth to us. So, while we may feel we're protecting ourselves with our masks, what's actually happening is that we're losing sight of our true selves. And how sad is that?

Now that we're collectively unmasking with our physical masks (finally), we suddenly feel a sense of vulnerability again. It's as though we're being reborn into a new world that we don't entirely recognize because it's not the same world it was before the pandemic. We're feeling around in the pitch-black trying to make sense of one another and our surroundings. Collectively, we're feeling disoriented. And if we don't first start by tuning into ourselves and taking off our figurative masks to locate our own starting point, we're going to be bumping into one another with reckless abandon. We can't see our own path forward until we find our internal compass. And we can't find our compass if we're not honest with ourselves about what is hidden behind our masks.

We live in a society that is running on empty. We're bumper cars motoring around blindly and chaotically, seeking one distraction after the next. This crazed, convoluted search for distractions stems from a need to avoid our very real feelings. People are chronically running away from themselves and wondering why they're feeling utterly lost and untethered. The truth is, you'll never find the answers to your feelings of emptiness and purposelessness by escaping yourself.

It's the search within, the unmasking of our false selves to find our true essence, that holds the answers that we seek.

So how do we unmask? Well, we first need to become aware that we're wearing a mask. Physical masks are obvious, but figurative masks—not so much. You can tell when you're wearing a figurative mask if you're holding yourself back, or if there are parts of you that you're withholding from yourself and/or others. If you're altering who you are around different people in your life or putting on a show instead of just being who you are, you're probably wearing a mask. If when you come home after a long day, you take a deep breath and finally allow yourself to exist as you naturally are, you've probably been wearing a mask all day. Basically, wearing a mask means not living in your full expression. It's a hinderance to the wholeness that is your natural self. And yes, it can be a terrifying thought to unmask. We live in a scary fucking world. But being afraid of your own inner self is the scariest thing of all. Because there's no such thing as escaping yourself.

The thing is, you cannot grow or live a full life with a mask on. You can live a pretend life, or a half-life, or a life prescribed to you by someone else. But it won't feel like your own. And just as putting on our physical masks became routine during the pandemic, our figurative masks become an automatic shield as well. You'll need to deliberately search for your mask and uncover the meaning behind it in order to free yourself. Perhaps the mask protected you from having to reveal something about yourself that you have a lot of shame around. Perhaps you're living in fear of showing your full self to the world because of past trauma. Whatever it is, you cannot begin your healing journey while still wearing a mask. The unmasking is what will allow you to see the truth that you're hiding from. Uncovering the mask will reveal to you what needs healing.

To heal and to live freely, you need space to breathe. You can't be simultaneously hiding yourself and finding yourself. If you're wearing a figurative mask, chances are you don't know who the "real you" is. You're pretending to be something you're not. You're running away from who it is you truly are. And the *only* way to reconnect with your inner truth is to remove your mask and start digging deep. The sooner we take off our figurative masks, the more connected we'll feel to one another, to ourselves, and most importantly—to our truth. If you're searching externally for the answers, you're looking in the wrong place. To re-enter the world without your mask will feel like an episode of Naked and Afraid, but the more honest you are with yourself, and the more you sit still in order to listen to your inner voice, the more you'll be able to trust your own light to guide you. It's time to collectively unmask.

Floating feelings
Filling up the endless expanse
Thoughts threading
Their way like the clouds
Out the foggy window
The gleaming glare
As the sun pokes through
Casting its light
On that blinding truth
Where the feelings reside
Somewhere deep inside
And as I sit amongst
Those puffed-up clouds
These feelings
Fill me, will me
To sit with them
And keep them company
As we float across the sky
Them and I.

The Truth Teller, on a flight home from San Diego, April 2022

CHAPTER 4

THE TRUTH ABOUT
INNER WORK

"There is no coming to consciousness without pain. People will do anything, no matter how absurd, in order to avoid facing their own soul. One doesn't become enlightened by imagining figures of light, but by making the darkness conscious."
— Carl G. Jung

So now that we've identified our figurative mask, let's discuss how the heck we do the work to toss it straight into the trash. We need to talk about what it means to do "the work." Since the start of the pandemic, there have been endless Instagram posts and TikToks about the importance of doing "the work," but a lot of people don't know what that means. And why would they? If you didn't grow up in a family that spoke about mental health or feelings in general, and no one around you did "the work," then you're not going to know what it really is or why you should be doing it. Moreover, we live in a society that needed a global pandemic to wake us up to the importance of our mental health. And that's a tragic truth. So instead of just telling you *that* you should do the work (which you ought to be doing if you're interested in living your most fulfilling life), we're going to begin by talking about what doing the work truly looks like.

Putting in the work is devoting time and energy to introspection about yourself and your past. It's about making connections between your thought patterns and behaviors. It's about uncovering the fundamental stories that have shaped you and understanding how one thing led to another in your life story thus far. It's about developing a solid understanding of yourself (which you are always building upon as you grow), so that you can live an authentic life that is truthful to who you are at your core. It's about developing a toolbox of healthy coping mechanisms that you can utilize when you're triggered instead of the abundance of easily accessible yet highly unhealthy coping skills that are always at our fingertips. Doing the work is a life-long investment in yourself. Choosing to do the work is a pivotal moment when you decide your life matters and that you're going to invest in it. And I'm not talking about investing in it financially. I'm talking about investing in it emotionally, with intention.

The inner work can be done in a variety of ways. Of course, there's talk therapy. As a therapist and someone who has been in therapy for years, I understand the significance and value of having an outside, unbiased perspective and a safe space to work through your innermost feelings. But there are other ways to do the work if therapy isn't an option or if it doesn't work for you. Journaling is a great way to get in touch with your feelings. Watching videos or reading books on certain topics you're struggling with is another. Making space for your emotions and actually *feeling* them is part of doing the work. There are all sorts of angles through which to approach this work. The important part is that you choose to do it.

If you don't "choose" to do it, life will choose for you, often when you have no other choice. Many people naively think they can go their entire lives without putting in this kind of therapeutic work. They bottle up their feelings that are way beneath the surface and gradually, they become more and more distant from their inner child and from all those around them.

But those feelings that you so badly want to convince yourself aren't affecting you are always at the steering wheel of your life, especially if you haven't worked through them properly. They're part of your story. And just like everyone else on this planet, we all have a past that informs our present. Unless you just popped out of the womb, you most likely have a story that needs to be unpacked and processed if you want to develop any understanding of who you are. Yes, you can live your life without doing the work. You can make the choice to never look within or to dig deeper. Flounder around on the surface if you so desire. But how's that serving you?

There are a lot of reasons why someone may choose not to do the work, or why they may avoid it at all costs. One is because, point blank, they're stubborn. They've already made up their minds and they aren't open to changing them. But if you feel the urge to grasp so tightly onto your viewpoints, you ought to ask yourself why. And perhaps when you take a look at it, you might realize that's the very thing you've been avoiding: to look within. To dig deeper. Maybe doing the work, or doing what's scary, will have payoffs that far outweigh the fear going into it. It's something to consider. Also, going to therapy doesn't mean you've "failed" or "given up." Quite the contrary. It means you've consciously chosen to work on yourself. You're taking responsibility for yourself and working to make your life, and the lives around you, better.

And yes, doing the work is a choice! It's a choice we all have. No, we don't all have the choice to go to therapy. The cost of and access to mental health treatment is a universal problem. But you can choose to do the work in other ways. Many people, and I call these people the "sleepwalkers," operate as if life is happening *to* them and they don't consider the prospect of becoming an active participant in their own life. They don't take accountability for themselves. They're asleep to themselves. They throw themselves in, but only partially. They live their lives placing value on things that, if they took a step back to consider them, they really don't give two fucks about. They're sad, they're angry, and they're lonely...and living a life they think is socially acceptable rather than one that would make them feel genuinely fulfilled. They carry other people's weight. They become codependent. Manipulative. Controlling. Threatening. Acting out all of their unhealed trauma. Projecting onto everyone else. Keeping themselves in unhealthy relationship cycles. Causing damage to those around them. All in the name of not doing "the work." Of not taking that real time-out to figure themselves out. Did you ever stop to think that choosing not to do the work is messy, irresponsible, and selfish when you're oozing out all your unwanted shit onto those around you?

The first time I went to therapy, I was thirteen years old. I'd heard of therapy, but I truly knew nothing about it. I thought it was for "crazy" people or people with huge life problems who couldn't "get it together." So, if this is what you think about therapy, know you are thinking like a naive thirteen-year-old girl in the early 2000s (LOL, #sorrynotsorry). So, it obviously wasn't my choice to go to therapy. In fact, I saw it as a punishment. My mom had encouraged me to go when I had a falling out with my best friend at the time. We were young, and I was the more outspoken and dominant one in the friendship. My best friend was shy and submissive, and as a result felt pushed around by me and felt like she had no voice. After having been best friends for four years and basically living at one another's houses, her mother called mine one day after school and informed her that her daughter no longer wanted to be friends with me because it was "too much." Of course, I took this to mean *I* was "too much" and "bad" and "wrong." At that age, it's difficult to understand that friendships end for a variety of reasons and that it's never just about one person. Also, things get skewed and lost in translation when you have a third party speaking on your behalf.

Anyway, I was distraught over this friendship breakup, so my mom suggested therapy. I was confused and deeply hurt. Why should *I* have to be the one to go to therapy when it wasn't me who did something wrong by ending the friendship? *I was the victim here!* Even as my mom expressed, on the way there, that the point of this was not to punish me but to give me insights and tools to work through the breakup that I was so depressed over, I still viewed the whole thing as a punishment. I was not thrilled about it, let's just say that.

I sat down on the couch as soon as I arrived at the office and, without even looking up at the therapist, the floodgates opened. I cried and cried and cried. For the entire session, I was wiping tears and apologizing for my tears. I don't even remember talking about the friendship much. I could hardly get a word out. I was so focused on the shame I felt about being in the therapy room that I was unable to focus on what I was there to talk through. This is what happens when you don't have a true understanding of therapy, or when you grow up in a society that doesn't value mental health the way it does other forms of health. I didn't personally know anyone else who went to therapy, and the only time I had seen it was in dramatized movies or television shows, and the client was always seemingly psychotic. If you had told me that one day I'd become a therapist, I would've looked at you as if you were insane.

But what happened, throughout my weekly sessions, was that I started to uncover certain truths about what led me to the therapy chair to begin with. I was able to process the friendship breakup and my feelings on it, as well as make sense of why it happened in the first place. I was able to draw connections between my own behaviors in the friendship and my behaviors in other relationships in my life. I recognized patterns that were working and those that weren't. I developed skills. I developed awareness. And I gradually found that therapy was not a punishment but a gift. So, my friend who ended the friendship maybe wasn't the one in therapy, but she also wasn't the one gaining imperative insight on herself that would help her in all her relationships to come. I was.

What many people don't realize is that feeling the deep, dark, complex emotions has incredible payoffs. People who are afraid of digging deeper are scared of what they will find if they really allow themselves to turn inward. Well, let me tell you a little something about feeling your feelings and digging deep: once you do so, your world opens up in an entirely new, beautiful way. You have a new lens of clarity through which to experience the world. You have more insight and meaning to pull from below the surface. Your relationships become richer. See, if you're distant with yourself, you're inevitably going to be distant with other people.

You can't build deep relationships with people who are running from their own depth.

You can live your whole life on the surface, but why would you want to? You don't even know how much you're missing out on in the way of deep, soulful connections and rich, wild love (with yourself and others). And #sorrynotsorry, that can't be accomplished if you're living life skimming the surface.

You can't Bubble Wrap your life by cutting yourself off from any real feelings and expect to live an authentic, beautiful existence. It just won't happen. Ironically, there's nothing "easy" about cutting yourself off from your true feelings, even though many of us like to convince ourselves otherwise. You're fighting an uphill battle. Your feelings aren't going anywhere. Those emotions you've stuffed down still exist, and they're growing every second that you turn a blind eye to them. You create inner turmoil when you neglect your true self in favor of sleepwalking through life. It takes way more effort to thwart your inevitable human experience than it does to just be who you are, say what you feel, and *feel* your feelings. You may feel "free" by not addressing your internal state, but you're actually just trapped behind lies, fear, and avoidance. True freedom comes from doing the work and learning what those limiting beliefs are so that you can work through them instead of being stuck and weighed down by their heaviness.

You can say you're fine without doing the work but let me ask you these questions: How well do you know what triggers you? How often do you allow yourself to sit with your emotions? Or to process them? Are the relationships in your life deeply fulfilling? Do you have a safe space to explore the complexities of your inner world without any biases or judgment? How well do you know yourself? Unless you can honestly say that you have a great grasp on who you are and feel fulfilled in that, you simply can't say that doing the inner work wouldn't *potentially* benefit you in some way. And listen, I'm not saying that therapy works for everyone. Again, therapy is only one way to do the work. What I am saying is that if you haven't ever been to therapy or done the work, then you can't possibly say for certain that it wouldn't help you. And as we know, there are millions of people who love to say this even though they're clearly not happy in the slightest.

The thing about doing the work is that it does require you to take accountability for yourself. When you avoid taking responsibility for who you are as a person, it inevitably gets in the way of your personal growth. What does it look like to take accountability for yourself? It looks like honoring yourself and your feelings by working on them. It means understanding that there are things within yourself that need to be worked through, and that you need to take ownership of those things in order to change them. It's understanding that doing the work is a choice and that you're having an impact on those around you when you choose *not* to do the work. Taking accountability will mean that there will be things you need to own about yourself that you might not want to take a look at. But maybe, in owning your part in your life, you'll feel empowered by it. Maybe you don't know unless you try.

Therapy is a secret weapon. It's secret because so many people still don't know how transformative it can be and what it can really do for an individual. It can profoundly impact many different aspects of your life. You'll never be working through only one problem. You'll be talking about your life as a whole. You'll gain clarity and perspective. You'll develop your own self-love and compassion. You'll undoubtedly find improvements in many areas of your life when you do this work. And if you aren't choosing to do the work, ask yourself why. What are you afraid of? What are you telling yourself about therapy? About doing "the work"? Is what you believe actually true? How do you know? Is there any other reason you're avoiding the work other than "it's hard" or you "have no time" or are "perfectly fine?" At the end of the day, if you aren't digging deep, your life will remain surface-level. And that's just the truth. Ultimately, the choice is yours: know yourself and thrive, or don't and just exist.

She picked up the block
Of sky-blue chalk as her bare knees
Scraped against the black concrete
Of the driveway, where, a few feet away
They all cluttered together
Picking teams, or so it seemed
She wasn't sure, as it didn't include her

So she clutched the brittle chalk
And she drew the boxes to play hopscotch
Perhaps, once they noticed her work
They'd ask her if they could join her
And so she kept her focus on the lines
She traced alongside her feet
As she heard their giggles and shrieks

One so loud she had to see
What it was she was missing
As she watched them all huddled around
A phone without a single sound
She looked back momentarily
At the empty boxes she had etched
A longing in her chest
Staring at them just hoping to feel seen
As they all stared at the screen.

The Truth Teller

CHAPTER 5

THE TRUTH ABOUT
SOCIAL MEDIA

"Sometimes the grass is greener because it's fake."
— @themindsjournal

We cannot discuss aligning with our inner truth without talking about the enormous machine that serves to suck all that truth right out of us: social media. Now, as much as I utilize social media both personally and professionally, I can also relate to the whole hate/love relationship many of us have with it. I know how my teenage patients feel when they are struggling to eat and seeing content on TikTok about how to starve themselves. I know the fear of having my own kids, one day, growing up with it and I'm sad they won't get to experience the 90's when social media hadn't yet taken over. I know how I personally feel when I see everyone's highlight reels on a day where that's the last thing I want to see. So, although I use social media daily, I dedicate my platform to spreading content that inspires and makes people feel seen. Because we need it. We have an abundance of filtered, fake content online and a severe lack of content that reflects reality.

We live in a culture of comparison. We compare our real, complex, layered lives to polished, well-edited highlight reels and wonder why we feel that something is "missing." We look towards influencers and celebrities to show and tell us how we should be structuring our days. And we take whatever they choose to show of their day at face value. If they say they're waking up at the crack of dawn and drinking a full glass of lemon water before a yoga flow and then journaling and meditating and making a healthy breakfast every single day, they must be doing that, right? (I know, I'm exhausted just writing that sentence. I can't imagine actually *living* that way.) We know it's not necessarily the truth, but we still allow ourselves to be influenced or even seduced by it. We attempt to model our days after these one-size-fits-all templates and feel like we did something wrong when we inevitably cannot keep it up. We think our lives would be better "if only" ours were more like so-and-so's. We continue to think this way even when we are proven wrong, continually. We see celebs and influencers speaking out about their sadness and grief and loneliness and hardships and we forget these things when we're staring at their glossy, heavily edited Instagram grids. Why do we do that? Because we aren't connected to our own truth.

Social media is certainly not the truth. And we spend more time scrolling than we spend sitting with ourselves. In other words, we spend more time living in a façade than we do in reality.

We need to talk about influencers, because truthfully, it's impossible to get to the heart of the issue here without it. My issue with influencers is that, oftentimes, they aren't genuine. And it's kind of the nature of the job. They aren't *required* to be genuine or to share their true selves with their followers (even though I'd argue that doing so would help them create stronger relationships with their audience). They're promoting products that they're being *paid* to promote. There *is* some ulterior motive here. And they signed up for that. But what gets confusing is when we are presented with influencers that wear a mask of authenticity. They *say* they are being vulnerable, because they know that that's what is being asked of them (and, frankly, that they will get "cancelled" if they aren't), but they only share half-truths or very tiny, filtered glimpses into their lives. And it's incredibly deceiving.

I'd venture to say that the large majority of influencers present a persona, or a mask, rather than their authentic selves. They share products that they clearly aren't genuinely using (who has a new hair product every week that is their "absolute holy-grail"?) and they give advice about things they've never personally experienced or been trained in. They think of authenticity as sharing *what* they are doing rather then *why* they are doing it and *how* it feels. (For example, sharing *that* you are moving across the country and painting it as a one-dimensional dream-like experience instead of sharing the reasons *why* you are moving and the inevitable stressors that come with a cross country move are two very different pictures to paint). And as much as we intellectually know this, we digest it in full and oftentimes forget what it is we are taking in.

Let's discuss an example of a common type of influencer we see on our explore page. This is the influencer who completely lacks authenticity. They do whatever they can to make their life appear "perfect," "flawless" and "enviable" to others. They are seemingly obsessed with creating an image of success. And listen, if you're that concerned with appearing successful, chances are it's because you don't feel that sense of success internally. In other words, you get your sense of self-worth from external validation because you don't feel valuable without the praise and adoration. Therefore, there is no real purpose or passion in anything this type of influencer is sharing. They often give off the impression that they're hanging on by a thread and that they're doing things not because they're truly passionate about them but for the accolades, exposure, and financial rewards. They're attached to outcomes and appearances. There is no foundation there. No reason other than the applause, which is not about their worth as a person but about the things they're promoting. How sad is that?

I don't say these things to "cancel" anyone. Or to "come for them." In fact, I see them as individuals who could seriously benefit from some introspection and doing the work. And as annoyed and frustrated as I get by them, they also make me very sad for them and about what they symbolize about our culture as a whole. My reason for discussing their problematic behavior is because we need to learn from those who we follow and are in the spotlight. We need to be aware of the direction in which our culture is moving. There are far too many young, impressionable people who take whatever is on their screens at face value and feel that they must act in the same way if they want the same results. The fact is, you can be *even more* successful doing something you are personally invested in than something you are after for the applause and "follows". The fact is that you're *not* seeing the full picture on social media, even when many influencers swear that they are being extremely transparent. We need to know what we are looking at. It doesn't mean we need to "cancel" people... you can't really cancel a human being, anyway. (And, truth be told, I think all of this "cancelling" is just a way for us to scapegoat and avoid the real underlying societal issues that need to be addressed, but I digress.) But you can make an educated decision on who to follow and be more cognizant of the impact that following certain individuals has on you.

If you're real with yourself, aren't the days you find yourself comparing to others the same days you are *already* having a rough day? Aren't you spending more time scrolling on your feed when you're *already* bored and lonely? We don't take into account that we are *already* feeling a certain way before we even begin the comparison process. And this is because most of us are out of touch with ourselves and don't have the awareness of where we end and the other person begins. We reach for our phones the second we open our eye-lids instead of allowing ourselves to... yup, you guessed it! Sit in the silence of our own thoughts and feelings. Most of us don't locate our own selves every morning before we locate what some stranger on Instagram or TikTok is doing with *their* morning. And that's a sad truth.

See, the more that you are in tune with yourself, and the more you have a clear concept of what you want to work on, the less you'll look to others for those answers. You'll realize that comparison is a pointless endeavor. It adds nothing to your life except FOMO and insecurity. You'll also realize that what you're comparing yourself to is not even what it seems. Are you posting pictures of your darkest moments? If the answer is "no" (which I'm sure for most of us it is), then why can't we understand that others do the same? We're all posting our highlight reels and then getting upset about other highlight reels wondering why they don't feel like *we* feel. But we aren't even posting all that we feel! Do you see the issue, here?

We all know the pros and cons of social media, so I won't get into that here. What I will say is I feel immensely fortunate to have grown up among the last generation before social media captured our youth. I spent my younger years playing hopscotch in the driveway and reading and writing and using my imagination to entertain myself. If I didn't have that time to figure out how to exist before a phone was shoved into my face and tried to tell me how to live my life, I'm sure I would've turned out much differently. But social media isn't going anywhere, so we must learn to live with it. Really, we must find a way to live with it without letting it destroy us in the process.

If we can't get rid of our feeds, we can minimize the power we give to them. We can spend less time scrolling. We can have more conversations about how Instagram is a false reality and that what we are seeing on there is simply not the full picture, or even an accurate picture at that. We can adjust our mindsets around social media. We can take inspiration from our *real* life, not just from what an influencer tells us they're doing (which they may or may not actually be doing). Since when are these influencers experts on what we should be doing with our own existence, anyway?

If there was any time it became more apparent that we shouldn't be looking to influencers as experts, it was during the pandemic. How many pseudo-doctors, "news anchors" and "therapists" did we see parading around on our feeds in the last few years? Far too many, let me tell you. And what's the issue with that, you ask? Well, when someone is presenting something as fact when it isn't backed by any true expertise, there's the obvious risk of spreading inaccurate information. People substituted getting their *actual* information with that from individuals who didn't know what they were talking about. Which is, of course, dangerous. As a therapist, I certainly found it quite amusing and highly frustrating to see people without any degree or experience of their own dolling out mental health advice. And what was frightening is how many people were listening and taking everything said at face value. News flash: just because someone has a platform doesn't mean they are an expert on every or any topic. It is, of course, understandable to want to have an authority to look towards for guidance, especially during such a complex and frightening time as a pandemic. But we need to be more discerning about *who* those authority figures are. And influencers? They're probably not your most accurate source of information when it comes to things like medical advice and psychology.

Truthfully, the "ideal" is different for everyone. We shouldn't be modeling our days after someone who isn't us to begin with! It might not be a good idea for us to wake up at 6 am and begin working out at 6:30 am on an empty stomach. In fact, given our own history, it may be very dangerous for us! It might not be a good idea for us to choose a more structured, time-sensitive form of therapy, like CBT (Cognitive Behavior Therapy) just because that is what is convenient for that particular influencer or celebrity. Perhaps a longer-form therapy—such as individual talk therapy—is what you need to truly work on yourself. And if we blindly adhere to the advice we get from those who aren't experts, we're setting ourselves up for disappointment and failure. We're not taking the time to consider what would *actually* be best for us personally. And that is one of the most problematic aspects of social media. It leaves us no room to think for ourselves.

That is, if we allow it to be that way. If we aren't doing the work or taking time to listen to our own thoughts, we will be even more susceptible to anything and everything outside of ourselves. Because if you don't know what your opinion is on something, but then an influencer tells you what to think, isn't it going to be pretty impossible to take a step back and form your own opinions from scratch? If you're not confident in yourself, and then you see someone parading around confidently on their feed, aren't you only going to feel worse? If you're overwhelmed by the thought of therapy and don't know where to begin, and you see an influencer on your feed swearing by a particular form of therapy, aren't you susceptible to just picking that instead of doing your own research? Of course, this certainly does not apply to everyone. I'd like to think we use our better judgment. But, truth be told, sometimes it's not about judgement. Sometimes it's an unconscious process and one that stems from true disconnection from our authentic selves and what we really need.

We're not gaining anything in actuality by copying or mimicking or curating our lives to look like anyone else's. We're only losing ourselves. We're shoving phones in our children's faces and wondering why they have no sense of self. You can't develop a solid sense of who you are when you're being presented with who you should be and given no time or opportunity to find who it is you truly are. We need to take a step back from our feeds and come up for air. We need to tune back into ourselves and tune out all of the noise. And we need to see it as that: it's just noise. It's fake, curated noise. And if you want to design your life based on someone's feed, you ought to take a stern look at yourself in the mirror and figure out how you're going to come back to you.

So, how do you come back to you? Stop automatically grabbing for your phone the second your eyelids open. Allow yourself a few moments to locate yourself. How do you feel? What sensations are going on in your body? Is there any tension? Any anxiety? Any lingering thoughts from yesterday or worries about today? Take this time for yourself, even if it's only a few minutes, before grabbing that phone. Do the same before you fall asleep. In fact, if you can, do something else besides scrolling before you shut your eyes at night. A good book is always a good idea. (Ahem!) Unfollow the accounts that don't speak to you or that don't add something helpful to your scroll. Take social media breaks. Have an internal dialogue with yourself while you are scrolling ("ugh, I know I'm seeing this influencer looking like she already accomplished ten things today while I'm still in bed" can be reframed as "okay, I'm still in bed and this person seems to be thriving. But maybe I needed the extra sleep. Maybe she's dealing with things that she isn't presenting to the world. Maybe I'm feeling vulnerable today and need to spend less time on my feed.") You get it. Don't disconnect from yourself while getting lost in your feed. Oh, and do that inner work.

The thing about social media is that it's not so black and white. There are horrible aspects of it, and there are very redeeming qualities about it as well. There's truth in both. It's about making it work for *you* in a way that aligns with your inner truth. And the more self-aware you are, the more you can create personal boundaries around social media that work for you. It's about knowing your limits and understanding how it impacts you when you see certain types of images or digest certain material. It's about honoring the space away from it you may need from time to time. It's engaging with it in a way that feels good to you. It might not be the same way your family and friends engage with it, and that's okay. You have your own truth. Listen to it.

Here's how I've made social media work for me. I have two accounts, my personal and my professional therapy account. My personal account is completely for fun. I post when I feel like it. I love creating photoshoots with cool backgrounds and figuring out where to put each image on the feed so that it all looks like a work of art. To me, it's like an adult art project that I can share with others. I've always felt very comfortable in front of the camera, and in fact I love being in front of the camera (you can trace this back to my acting days and the fact that my dad took awesome home videos of my brother and I from a young age. Oh, and I'm super confident. We'll get to that). Then, my professional account is @thattrendytherapist. I use that to share my daily truth bombs and insights. And having these two separate accounts works very well for me. On Trendy, I follow others in the field or related fields that have pages aimed to inspire and spread awareness. And it's amazing to see that there are others like myself who do use their pages to make others feel more connected. Although I don't set actual time-limits on my phone, I'm very aware of when I've been scrolling for too long and need to come back to myself. I always keep in mind that what I'm seeing online is purely a highlight reel. It's an enjoyable creative outlet for me, and a place where I can build my professional brand, but I don't at all get it confused with what's important: my real life.

We need to conceptualize social media as being separate and apart from our inner truth. Because it is. And if we don't know what that truth is, we need to start connecting with that before we get lost in the scroll. We need to remember the life that existed long before social media was introduced. We need to remember that we *can* survive without it. It's not that we need to stop using it altogether. But we need to adjust the *way* that we are using it. Otherwise, social media will become our youth. It already has its grip on the minds of our youngest generations. So, before you stick that first iPhone in your children's hands, make sure they've learned to play with chalk.

Smile, he said, as the camera clicked
And she lifted the corners of her lips
On cue just like she knew to do
"How beautiful!"
If only he really knew
As he peered into her eyes
Utterly mesmerized by the lies
Not knowing what hid behind
That smile, so empty yet so wide
But she was terrified
That perhaps he could see the truth
That hid behind the mask she packed
For whenever she was asked
To smile back, but only for the flash
And that was that.

The Truth Teller

CHAPTER 6

THE TRUTH ABOUT
POSITIVITY

"I don't believe our world needs more positivity. I believe our world needs minds that are equipped to be with the complexity of life. Minds that can hold nuance and polarity. Minds that can stay grounded, centered, and open to the full range of what it means to be human."
— Cory Muscara (@corymuscara)

So, there's another kind of mask we've not yet touched on: the "positivity" mask. This mask is worn by the person who claims to be all "love and light." You're probably chuckling to yourself because someone came to mind, or maybe you're the person wearing this mask. The "positivity" mask is worn by the person who only has time for what makes them smile. They're enthusiastic. They're often the life of the party. They get everyone going. They're usually quite fun to be around. So, what's this mask hiding? Well, they're often driven by an intense fear of deprivation. On the surface, it just looks like they're here to spread joy and have a great time. And yes, in part, that's true. But the underlying motivation for the constant need for pleasure is often a lack of nurturance in their upbringing. They realized along the way that they were in charge of nurturing themselves. They developed a fear of missing out. Yes, FOMO. They preach "good vibes only," because they're avoiding anything that isn't light and joyous. They're immensely afraid of having to face their own shadow. They're afraid to be bored. They're afraid to sit with themselves for fear of what might surface because they don't think they can tolerate it. They're continually looking for a way out, or an escape. An escape from the dull parts of life and the darkness that exists within themselves. And, thus, they become toxically positive.

We've all heard of "toxic positivity." And, perhaps, those of us who identify as glass-half-full people have wondered how positivity can be attached to such an ugly word as "toxic." We accept this false and faulty idea that being positive will dissolve all of life's worries and bring everyone together in a harmonious dance. "If only" we could all be more positive, then the world would be permanently cloaked in joy, right? And when we start to question positivity, we're labeled as "negative" and viewed as if something is fundamentally wrong with us. Ironically, we never question why many people who describe themselves as "positive people" are still seemingly empty and unhappy. We never talk about what is missing in those who preach positivity as if their lives depend on it. *Hmm, why do they depend on it?*

As we know, many people make it their mission to "just be positive." Although I've never described myself as a "positive person," it's not that I'd describe myself as being "negative" either. I'd say I'm a realist because I'm interested in the truth, whether that truth is perceived as positive or not. Yes, being able to look on the "bright side" of things can be helpful, but positivity has many blind spots. Life isn't all about slapping on a smile and getting jiggy with it, hate to tell you. Sometimes, and oftentimes, positivity is a mask we wear to protect us from the *real* work and introspection that needs to be done. Moreover, positivity becomes toxic when it invalidates the unique emotional experience of the individual. I'll elaborate.

There are a handful of people I know who are toxically positive. They wear their positivity like a badge of pride. I've found that while I enjoy the energy and optimistic outlook of these individuals, there's a limit as to how deep my relationships with these types of people can go. Because, of course, they can't tolerate anything other than the fluff. And I'm not all about the fluff, obviously. There was an instance when one of these individuals hurt me, and I tried to have a conversation with them about it. When I expressed my feelings, they actually laughed at me. The message was loud and clear: that I should just quit being "negative" and put on a smile. (Anyone who tells you to just "smile" as if that's life's cure for everything has a mountain of work to do, but I digress.). The issue is that they didn't actually *listen* to what I was saying or truly care about how their actions made me feel. They had no time for it and just wanted me to get over it. And, of course, that's toxic. Because what it told me is that in order to get along with them, or to continue the relationship, I had to neglect my true feelings (because clearly, they weren't willing to do any real introspection on their part). There was no real communication or comprehension happening on their end. So, the only way to continue my friendship with them was to neglect how I was feeling and continue to roll with the punches. And I wasn't about to roll with those punches.

The problem, then, with living life in "la la land" is that life just isn't that way. So, the escapist continues to run away and they never face what desperately needs to be worked on. They think they can outrun their pain. But then, they never learn how to deal with it. They don't develop the necessary experience and insights that come from sitting with difficult emotions and reflecting on them. They become flooded with panic whenever they're called on to sit still. They chase "happiness" as if it's a destination. And they never reach it, of course. Because happiness only exists in the present. And since they're always busy planning the next thing, they never get to feel the joy that's around them at any given moment. They'll wake up one day and wonder why they've done all of these exciting things in their life but they're still feeling empty. Because the actual living of life passed them by.

We call it "toxic positivity" for a reason. It's toxic to expect positivity from ourselves and others when a situation clearly evokes other kinds of feelings. Sometimes, you don't feel positive. In fact, most often, we don't wake up with a grin glued to our face. We fake it. We become it. We deliberately *choose* it. We force the positivity upon ourselves because we're told it's what we need to do to be "good people." But is it? Is it being a "good person" when a loved one tells you your actions have hurt them and you choose to ignore them because you want to avoid what you see as "negativity"? Again, let's think more deeply here. What are we missing by being positive? Well, quite frankly, we're missing a heck of a lot. The message of "be positive" is as vague as the words "mean" and "nice" (more on that soon). It's not really saying anything except shut up and deal with it, and also look on the bright side. News flash: life's not all about the bright side.

Life's about being real about what's happening. It's not about trying to morph every experience into a one-dimensional grin and acting as if we don't have any worries or doubts. What's so problematic about telling someone to be positive? Beyond the fact that it's an over-simplification of feeling and experience and doesn't hold any real meaning, it makes people feel like their authentic feelings are invalid or wrong in some way. It makes people feel as if something is fundamentally wrong with them if they can't seem to approach life with an unrelenting smile. What if you *can't* be positive? What if you have feelings that would be considered "negative" by the general population? Well, we *all* have those feelings. And, truth be told, there are no negative or positive feelings, and we need to stop labeling them as such. The labeling is toxic in and of itself. Every feeling has a place and a purpose. And if we're just blindly told to "be positive," we're getting the message that our individual feelings don't matter. We're being denied our very real human experiences and are made to question them and what they say about us when we're simply told that positivity is the only way. Moreover, by encouraging people to be positive and shaming them out of any alternative emotion, we're sending the message that the world has no space or time for you if you're struggling or in pain. It's sending the message that "if it's not positive, we don't want to hear it." And that's inherently problematic. (And we wonder why so many of us don't feel heard or understood in our daily interactions.)

Truthfully, the people who wear their "positivity" masks aren't very grounded in reality. They're hovering over it, looking for the next best thing on the horizon. In fact, they're usually the people who are cut off from themselves and out of touch with the world as it is. They're disconnected from themselves and others. They're unwilling to see the reality of life, which is full of both light and darkness. And, thus, they're not "full" or "whole" individuals.

To be a whole person, you must embrace the light *and* the dark and integrate them both into your being.

It's precisely the people who tell you to "be positive" that have no tolerance for life's inevitable darkness. They don't *want* to see it. They don't think they can handle it. They're *afraid* to allow themselves to feel anything other than "positivity," whatever that means. And, therefore, they don't want you to see it either. If you see it, it might force them to face their reality, too.

It's not that we shouldn't find ways to make the best out of situations. Heck, if we didn't do that, none of us would have made it through the pandemic without being destroyed in the process. But we need to be realistic about our outlook on life, and we also need to make room for the plethora of feelings and experiences that life holds. Life isn't all rainbows and butterflies, obviously. So why are we pretending it is? Why are we making people feel ashamed when they're not performing positivity for the world? The truth is that positivity *is* often a performance. It's an act. "Act more positive." Positivity is not a feeling. It is a way of being, and oftentimes it is a coping mechanism that one adopts in order to shield oneself from painful feelings and experiences. And, sure, there's a time and a place for that added layer of protection. But to make it your life's way is to neglect the many real aspects of life. It's to avoid reality.

The reality is that life's problems cannot simply be fixed with a positive attitude. That's literally just slapping on a Band-Aid and neglecting what is *actually happening* around us and within us. We're neglecting the inner work that needs to be done in favor of acting like we're happy about things when we clearly are not. Being positive isn't going to wash away your worries. They'll still be there until you sit with them and figure out how you truly feel about them. As much as we may want to believe, there are no short cuts to the inner work. The only way through it is to literally move through it.

POSITIVITY

There's nothing wrong with you if you don't consider yourself to be a positive person. Understand that the message of "be positive" is limiting, invalidating and unrealistic. No one feels positive all the time. It's just not possible. It's actually a lie. You're not fooling anyone by pretending everything is sunshine and all is well in the world. All is not well. If it were, our world wouldn't be broken and in need of building back up. So, to simply say "be positive" is both avoiding doing anything to help drive change and inhibiting those who understand fundamentally the need to feel the fullness of their human experience. We need people who can see into the darkness and help us navigate it. These are the truth tellers. Without them, life is surface level and a performance and holds no real meaning.

If you don't wake up every day feeling positive, or even if you go weeks at a time without feeling positive, it doesn't mean anything is wrong with you. Don't let people who are afraid to look at their own darkness make you feel wrong for your valid human experience. You can't get to the light without first sitting with the dark, anyway. That's why you often see so many people who preach being positive having empty existences. They don't feel fulfilled because they're not, and they can't be. You can't be fulfilled if you're not embodying the full truth of what it means to be human. Sometimes, you'll feel positive. Other times, you won't. That just means you're really living. Do you want to live, or do you want to pretend? I'll let you answer that.

Every syllable I utter is
Scoffed at and stifled
Can't find a breath
Frozen in a fog of fear
Trying to dissolve
Little bullets digging into
Open wounds
Causing a tornado inside me

They light me on fire
Then blame me for burning
And I stand here
Back against the wall
While they all have their free for all
They create a mockery of me
Then judge me for breaking free.

The Truth Teller

CHAPTER 7

THE TRUTH ABOUT
BEING "NICE"

"The people who are nice to you aren't always being kind to you. Saying what you want to hear is nice. People sugarcoat feedback to make you feel good today. Sharing what you need to hear is kind. People speak honestly to help you do better tomorrow. Candor is an act of care."
— Adam Grant (@AdamMGrant)

L et's talk about one of the common conundrums we face when it comes to bringing our inner truths out into the open. We're told we need to be "nice." How many times have you been told to "be nice"? How many times have you seen someone's Instagram bio read something like "above all, be kind" or "kindness is cool"? I'm sure it's too many times to count. We started hearing these phrases from our elders in early childhood and have been reminded of the importance of kindness ever since. Let me start by saying this: yes, being kind is important. We should all strive to be kind. No one is debating that here. The discussion here is not about *whether* we should be kind. But there's a distinct difference between being "nice" and being "kind" that we need to address. And, furthermore, we need to really consider the overemphasis and overvaluation of being "nice" above all else, especially when it comes at the expense of being unkind to ourselves. We need to pay attention to our true motivations when we're being "nice." We need to consider the fact that when you're making your Instagram bio "in a world where you can be anything, be kind," or telling your friend you don't like what they're saying and that they should be nicer, you're not saying much at all.

Truth be told, to be considered a "nice" person, all one must do is put on an act. Being "nice" in our society means being agreeable, performing pleasantries, and not causing a ruckus. Truthfully, being "nice" is incredibly easy. Because to be nice, you don't need to have the actual intentions of kindness. You can just hold that door open or say "please and thank you" when the time calls for it. We can *all* do these things. But do these behaviors mean that we are coming from a place of true kindness? Not in the slightest. We can do the thing that everyone else would consider "nice," while simultaneously feeling entirely different inside. For example, you can thank someone for a gift that you don't like. You can include someone whom you don't actually care for. You can say "please" just because you don't want to get yelled at for being "rude." But none of this means you have a genuine heart with pure intentions. It just means you're doing what society expects of you. Period. And that's really all it takes to be considered "nice."

Let me elaborate. The words "nice" and "mean" are subjective. *I know, a wild concept.* While we can universally agree on many actions and behaviors that would fall under each category, the meaning of these words is quite vague. What you find nice may not be what I think of as nice. For example, you might think it's "nice" to accept an invitation to someone's party who has been gossiping about you to others who will be there. Maybe you think it's nice because you've been taught that what's more important than your own self-respect is to do whatever you can to make other people happy. But is it really nice to put yourself in a situation with someone who has disrespected you? If you were to take a second to ask your inner child this question, I'm pretty damn sure you'd get a resounding "no." So by simply using the words "nice" and "mean" to try and tell someone how to behave differently, we're not expressing our true needs. We're using these labels as placeholders for our underlying feelings. Think about it: it's far easier to tell someone you think they're being "mean" instead of explaining to them specifically *how* what they've said or done has impacted you. Furthermore, we overuse these words. We say them *all the time.* Anything said that often, especially words that bring us back to the kindergarten playground, lose their meaning. So, know that when you're telling someone to "be nice," not only do you sound annoying and preachy, but you haven't actually communicated exactly what you want from the other person at all.

There are lots of reasons why people overuse these phrases. First, they're easy. It takes less than two seconds to utter the words "be nice." People love these catchall phrases that they think will lead to great change. They love them because they're safe and think they can't be debated. Second, many people like to have a firm structure as a way to define themselves as a "good" or "bad" person (and further, it's a simple way to place others in those same categories). These are the people who feel it is more important to be *seen* as "good," *even* when that might come at the expense of true honesty. Well, guess what? Being dishonest isn't nice, no matter how you slice it. And if your life motto is "be nice" at all costs, then you haven't really thought too deeply about things. Let me ask you something: When have you ever been told to just "be nice," and it completely snapped you out of whatever mood you were in and suddenly everything was all glitter and gold? I mean, if that's happened to you, good for you. But I can tell you, all I've ever experienced is people using that phrase to shut others up, control them, guilt them, try to make them feel badly, or dismiss them altogether.

Here's the thing: if you feel you must do things to prove you are a "nice person," then understand your motivation isn't kindness.

Because if you were truly a good person, you wouldn't feel the constant need to prove it. You wouldn't feel that urge to make a TikTok or Instagram story every time you do a good deed. (And, while we're at it, let's stop pretending as if sharing these "good deeds" is motivated by inspiring others. We all know how to do a good deed, thank you very much.) If you're truly acting from a place of kindness, then it won't even occur to you to promote it to others. If you're truly a "good person" who acts out of the kindness of their soul, you don't feel the need to shout it from the rooftops. People don't need to witness your acts of kindness for them to matter. In fact, they matter more when they stay between you and the recipients of your kindness. Because it means your intentions were pure.

What is truly nice consists of kind motivations. If you're being "nice" because you want to consider yourself a "good person," then it's not coming from a place of genuine kindness. It's performative. It's self-serving to make yourself feel better, or to act as if you're doing the "right thing." For example, let's say you go to someone's party whom you don't like. Perhaps you got the invitation, and you have nothing else to do that night. And all your other friends are going. So, you decide to go purely for those reasons. Oh, and because you don't want to suffer FOMO. But how about the message that sends to the person hosting the party? They don't know your underlying motivations. They assume that since you're showing up, you want to be there. That you guys are on good terms. But then when you're at the party, you're on your phone the whole time and barely say two words to the host. (Again, you don't truly want to be there, so you're doing whatever you can to pass the time.) The host sees this and is confused and hurt. They don't understand why you'd make the effort to show up when you're not even interacting with them or acting as if you want to be there. So, by you showing up with ulterior motivations, you're causing someone else pain. That's obviously not nice. It's fake and deceiving. We can all "act" nice. That doesn't count as actual kindness. Motivations matter, people. It's never "nice" to act as if you're coming from an altruistic place when that just isn't the truth.

We also tend to carelessly throw around the term "mean" when we don't like someone's actions. We do this, oftentimes, without even knowing the motivations behind these "mean" actions. Truth be told, it's unfair and manipulative when someone calls you "mean" just because you had enough respect for yourself to walk away from a situation where you were not being treated well. End of story. There's nothing "nice" about staying in a relationship with someone (friend, family, or otherwise) that is disrespectful to you or who has wronged you repeatedly. All you're doing is showing yourself that you have no standards in terms of how you want to be treated, and you're simultaneously showing others they can treat you however they want, and you'll just swallow it because it's the "nice" thing to do. Is that really the world we want to live in? A world where we deem others "kind" for keeping the peace at all costs and remaining in unhealthy relationships? I can tell you it's not how I operate, and it's not how anyone who has any desire to live a life of authenticity and self-respect operates either.

See, if we tell someone they aren't being nice, or even worse, that they're "not a nice person" (which is a character assassination), we're tacking a label onto them so that we don't have to deal with the feelings they inspire in us. For example, maybe your friend said something you didn't like or agree with. If you just decide your friend is a "mean person," then you can use that to justify to yourself (and to your family and friends) why you're not hanging around with them anymore. But labeling someone a "mean person" is never the full story. In placing these labels on others, we're overlooking the many nuances that are inherent in our own humanity. To say that someone as a whole is "mean" is to disregard the complexities that are part of human nature. Someone can say something that hurts you without it automatically meaning that the wholeness of their being is "bad" or "wrong" or "cruel." Have you ever said something to someone that might be considered mean? Of course you have. *We all have.* And unless we are ax-murderers here (and if you are, how on earth did you get a copy of my book?) we shouldn't be labeling people as "good" or "bad" based on whether we like or dislike their behavior. It's not up to us to place these labels on others, and frankly, they can have completely damaging effects.

Here's the truth: people who tell you to be nice aren't always considering whether you're being nice to *yourself.* It isn't being nice to yourself to neglect your own needs just to meet those of others. You're not being nice to yourself if you hold back your feelings just because you're afraid of upsetting someone. It's not nice to go to someone's party whom you don't like but are afraid to upset. None of that is nice! And it's manipulative to make someone *think* that these things constitute universally nice behavior. And, hello, we cannot be nice to anyone unless we're nice to ourselves first and foremost. And when we throw around these "nice" and "mean" labels, we're forgetting that people internalize them, and then they start to feel a certain way about themselves that may not be true. And the consequences of internalizing these labels can be extremely tragic. This happened to me back in high school when I developed my eating disorder. I stopped speaking my truth so openly. I restricted myself. I ended up harming myself because I was afraid to allow my full, true self to exist, because I didn't want others to get the wrong impression about me if I looked at them in the "wrong" way or had a certain tone in my voice. The point is you don't know the effect you're having on someone by the kindergarten name-calling. It's not proving the point you think it is, and it may cause way more harm than you could fathom.

If you have the urge to tell someone to "be nice," take a step back and consider why you're wanting to say that and what you're actually trying to convey. Truthfully, it's far more effective to communicate to someone what, specifically, has bothered you rather than calling them a juvenile name. Also, understand that there may be more to the story. At first glance, you might think it's "mean" that your friend decided not to attend their upcoming family event. But perhaps he's coming from a place of maintaining his inner peace and self-growth. Perhaps he's making an intentional choice not to be in an environment that doesn't align with who he is as a person. Maybe by not going to the event, he's being kind to his inner child who respects himself and his values over making the choice that would appease others. And guess what? It isn't for you to determine whether he's right or wrong about that (or even whether it's "mean" or "nice" of him). Because there is no right or wrong! It's his *truth*. And his truth is that, for whatever reason, he knows better than to put himself in an unhealthy environment. So instead of calling him "mean" and recruiting others to think he's "mean" (which can be considered immature behavior that further confirms he's made a great choice for himself), ask yourself: Why does it bother me? Is there something triggering to you when someone turns down an invitation to somewhere they're expected to be? Or do you just want something to gossip about? Or can you not fathom being that in tune with yourself that you can put up those bold boundaries like he does? He's being nice to himself. You should try it, too.

We need to adjust what we think of as being "nice." Instead of using a vague, four-letter word we learned as one of our first words here on earth, let's get more advanced in our definition. Ultimately, we should strive to come from a place of truth and honesty. We should strive to love ourselves fully and to express that full self to the world without any apologies. Of course, we should be mindful and respectful of others, as well. But we can't— and shouldn't—try to control or manipulate others by labeling them as "mean" when we don't like what they're doing or saying. How can you possibly pretend that *that* is nice?

So, let's talk about what it really means to "be kind," so that when we toss around that phrase we use it correctly. And also, so that we can stop misinterpreting someone's "nice" gestures for being a genuinely kind person. Being kind means to be authentic and honest with yourself and others. It means showing up fully as yourself in your relationships and putting in the real effort that is required in any healthy relationship. Being kind means to be thoughtful, empathetic, loyal, intentional, and trustworthy. It means keeping your word and helping others out of the pure goodness of your heart, not because you expect something in return. It means being kind not only when times are good but when times are rough. It means having integrity. It means communicating directly to someone when there is an issue instead of talking behind their back or lazily throwing around character assassinations such as "mean" or "rude." You cannot consider yourself kind if you're not doing these things. Kindness requires realness. Kindness requires truth.

Kindness is important...when it's coming from a place of truth. We cannot let being nice be at the expense of being real. We cannot continue to label others as "mean" or "nice" as a way of getting our own personal needs met. We need to honor the fullness and depth of our humanity that cannot be boiled down to one word labels about our true nature. We need to stop telling people they're mean when they're just speaking their truth. We need to stop with the toxic positivity and over-generalizations that the ultimate goal is for everyone to be nice all the time. The ultimate goal is to live out our truth and form relationships with ourselves and others based on that truth. And you can't possibly determine what someone else's truth is unless you've taken the time to ask them, or unless you've taken a walk in their shoes. That can't be accomplished by calling them "mean." Let's leave those basic words at the playground and say what it is we genuinely want to convey. Oh, and before you make your Instagram bio or your life's slogan some iteration of "be kind above all else," make sure your intentions are in the right place. Otherwise, it ain't kindness. It's just a performance.

Color me black
Speckle me with projections
The discarded pieces
You keep hidden
Tucked away somewhere
In the dusty corners of your soul
Aim those misperceptions
Right at me like little bullets
Each one loaded with your
Unwanted shame and pain
Anything you can do
To unburden yourself
While burdening me
Until you feel a false sense
Of power, while I
Stand in the darkest depths
Of your projected fragments
Wading through a war of words
That are not my own
As I try to parse through them
To locate what is mine
And the fire in me fizzles
Sizzling away at the mass of black
That you think I cannot crack
Casting light on your shadows
And at once, your black
Reflects back
Color me black

The Truth Teller

CHAPTER 8

THE TRUTH ABOUT
BEING LIKED

*"You are not for everyone, and you
were never supposed to be."*
— *Africa Brooke*

N ow that we've discussed our desire to be seen as "nice,"
let's zoom outward and consider the broader desire we
have, societally, to be "liked." We're far too concerned
with being "liked." We live in a world that places an inordinate
amount of emphasis on being "liked." We're taught to prioritize being "liked." We're taught to do whatever it takes to be a
"nice person" so that we *will* be "liked." We're desperate to get
others to like us as if that's where our self-worth should stem
from. What we forget is the part about liking *ourselves* and the
fact that there's no actual possibility of everyone liking you. It's
simply unrealistic. Because, truthfully, you don't even like everyone, do you?

So, let's start this chapter here: the first issue with "being
liked" is the over-valuation of getting people to like us at the
expense of ourselves. We shouldn't be getting our sense of self-
worth from whether others like us. Someone can choose not to
like you because your bold personality reminds them of their
third cousin's boyfriend's sister, who said that "mean" com-
ment to them four years ago and now they associate everyone
with a bold personality with that person. And, of course, there
is literally nothing you can do about that! It's a projection, and
one that reveals far more about the other person than it does
about you.

Oftentimes, we automatically determine how we feel about a person before we actually get to know them. We decide, unconsciously, how we feel and then view all subsequent information through that limited lens. Or we put people in boxes. We decide which kind of people we associate with and who we avoid like the plague. Of course, it's great to have standards and values when it comes to who you want to interact with. But some people get far too rigid about these labels, and they're unwilling to take in new information to see things differently. And if you're not open to taking in new information about a person and changing your mind as you integrate this new information, then what are you really basing your opinion on?

The truth is that people can say they like you without genuinely knowing who you are. Conversely, people will decide they don't like you for reasons that have nothing at all to do with you. People try and convince themselves, or decide consciously, not to like you for so many different reasons that have absolutely nothing to do with who you truly are. Why? Because it's *easy*. Then they don't have to make the effort to actually get to know you. And what you'll find, most times, is that the people who say they don't like you are the ones who don't know the first thing about you. A lot of the time, people think they don't like you based on information they've been told by *other* people who've decided not to like you. Or people tell themselves they don't like you because their insecurities are triggered when they're in your presence. And instead of taking a closer look at *why* they are hurt, and where it stems from in their *own* history, they cast all the blame onto you. We need to quit taking it at face value when someone says they don't like us. There's always more to the story that most likely has nothing to do with you.

Let's also recognize the fact that it doesn't really take much for people to say that they *do* like you. People who think in black-and-white terms take the smallest gestures to mean that someone fits in their distinct boxes of "good guy" or "bad guy." If someone smiles in your direction, for example, you might consider them a "good person" simply from an optics stand-point. But let's not forget that you can smile at someone who you don't actually like just to appear as if you're doing the "right thing," as we went over in the previous chapter. And does that mean that you're being kind, or just that you're doing what is apropos? *You already know the answer.* Also, how would you feel if someone smiled at you whenever they saw you and you later found out from someone else that they didn't really like you? Wouldn't that be confusing and hurtful?

The issue with our overwhelming desire to be liked and to "do the right thing" is that it masks true intentions (a.k.a. our inner truths). Let's say you just had an argument with a friend, and you're still hurting. You and this individual have a rocky history, and the argument was the last straw. You feel extremely uncomfortable around them, but now you have to see them at a mutual friend's birthday party. Now, your inner truth is probably screaming in your ear how you really feel about this person and the fact that you don't want to see them. And, if you have to see them, you don't want to interact with them in any way because you're still hurting. You intend to go to the party and be cordial but keep your distance. Fair. Valid. But, because societally, we place such emphasis on being liked, we may feel pressure to be fake so as not to stir up any drama (we don't know how this person will react if we don't perform the appropriate pleasantries—which shouldn't be our problem—but I digress). But there's a difference between starting drama and simply choosing not to engage with someone who you're not comfortable around, for good reason. In these situations, we're expected to do what goes against our better judgment. We force ourselves to be pleasant towards this person at the party for the sake of everyone else. And because we don't want to be disliked. But it's not because we genuinely want to. We're completely disregarding our gut instincts for the sake of the crowd. As if it's "wrong" or "mean" to simply co-exist at a party with someone you are not on good terms with.

Also, let's really consider this. Does giving someone a fake smile or embrace, when you don't feel comfortable doing so, automatically make you a good person? No. It simply means you are doing what is expected of you, probably to avoid conflict (if you're being honest). Intentions matter. If your definition of someone who is likable is limited to the pleasantries they perform, then you really ought to take a closer look at how you define a "good person" and why you are overlooking the underlying motivations behind those pleasantries. Because it's dangerous to assume someone is a good person just because they play the role that is expected of them. You might be keeping people close to you that aren't genuine. Truthfully, it's simply deceptive to act one way when you feel entirely different internally.

When you're in a situation where you don't feel completely safe to be yourself, or when you know you're not respected, you're probably not going to let those people see the real, full you. Why would you? You don't feel safe or comfortable. Personally, I'm not the type of person to act like we're on good terms when we're not, because that's misleading and inauthentic. I wouldn't like it if someone acted one way towards me when we are together, just to "be nice," but acted differently when we are apart. I respect myself enough not to put myself in situations with people who don't respect me. I don't feel safe in situations where I can't be my complete self without being disrespected or made to feel badly in some way. I value liking myself over others liking me. And that's just the truth.

The root of someone's dislike for another is also important to consider. If you think or say you don't like someone without trying to understand them or their point of view, then you need to get real with yourself. Do you really know them? Have you taken the time to get to know them? Or have you allowed your preconceived notions, the judgment of others, or gossip about another person to influence your perceptions of them? Here's the thing: life's not just about playing along and being "nice" in order to be liked by others. It's *deeper* than that. I'd rather be nice to myself and not harm myself by putting myself in situations that I don't feel safe in—for good reason—than *appear* nice to others while abandoning my inner child. Because what is it really accomplishing to *appear* nice, anyway? Nothing at all.

The deeper issue with being liked by everyone is the fact that you can't actually do that without abandoning yourself in the process.

The goal should be liking yourself. And, sadly, many people never achieve that goal because all of their focus is on getting others to like them at their own expense.

There are many reasons why you might say that you don't like someone. And most of the time, it's not the actual *person* you dislike, but rather the *feeling* that person inspires in you. Perhaps that person has done a lot of inner work, while you've pushed down your feelings, trying to escape them. Or maybe you've been taught to people-please and "go with the flow," and this person tells it like it is and doesn't focus on keeping the peace. Whatever it is, instead of being curious about *why* we feel the way we do around certain people, we decide we don't like them. That way, we don't have to deal with the complexity of feelings that person brings out in us. Or, even better, we get others to agree with us and decide not to like this person as well. Misery loves company, right? Hating on others makes you feel good, right? It's a sad, sad truth that many live by.

At the end of the day, there are going to be people who dislike you for listening to and acting on your internal instincts instead of the role that's expected of you. There will be people who will call you "mean" and not like you for simply putting yourself first and stating your truth. The reality is that they don't know how to be "nice" to themselves, so of course, they can't fathom why you're not playing along like they do. Truthfully, the more you like yourself, the less you'll need others to like you. It doesn't mean that other people *won't* like you once you like yourself. Chances are that more people will genuinely like you because you're being your authentic self. And when you are coming from a place of self-love, you won't feel the need to please people in the way that you do when you don't love yourself. Needing people to like you comes from a lack of self-love. If you lack love for yourself, you may feel an overwhelming need to get that love externally. But then it's not genuine. It's just another need being fulfilled. It's dependency. And other people can feel that. It feels like they're being used. It feels fake and as if it lacks substance because it does. When you truly love yourself, being liked by other people becomes a bonus. It's no longer a need but a real connection stemming from a place of truth. So, shift your focus. Do *you* like you?

If you're "for everyone" then you've got to take a step back and wonder why and what that says about you. It either means you're putting on a performance to get everyone to like you, or you're suppressing your true nature. You shouldn't *want* to be liked by everyone. Because if you are, that means you're probably keeping your life surface-level and withholding certain aspects of yourself that you're too afraid to show. It means you're wearing a mask. You're not expressing your honest opinions because you're afraid of disagreement, which means you're playing life safe and small. Life isn't about getting everyone to like you. And if you're prioritizing everyone liking you at the expense of being who you are in full, then truthfully, you probably don't like yourself.

Truthfully, we should be aiming to be *valued*, not liked. Being liked just isn't that deep. You can say you like someone whom you've never even met before. Like celebrities. But being valued is when someone truly knows who you are and likes that person. You have to genuinely know a person in order to understand what it is you value about them. Being liked is not the same thing as being loved. You can be liked by people by performing pleasantries that our society deems as "polite," but those pleasantries exist only on the surface. They don't say much of anything about your intentions or true nature. Being valued is where it's at. It means others will miss or crave your presence when you're not around. And if your presence is simply politeness and fading into the background, then there's nothing at all to miss.

If it's your goal to be liked by everyone, ask yourself this: If everyone likes you, what does that *really* say about you? Perhaps it's not the badge of honor you'd like to think it is. Maybe it means you're too accommodating and don't stand up for yourself. Maybe it means you don't have strong opinions or are afraid to vocalize them. Maybe it means you don't value your own needs or desires. Maybe you're living out of fear and are afraid to disrupt the peace. Are any of those worthy "goals?" It's a warped idea to think that everyone should like you, and, frankly, it's not a useful "goal" at all. To be liked by everyone means that you'll have to dull out the parts of yourself that would make people love you. The only way to guarantee that you're liked by the majority is to quiet your own uniqueness. And in doing so, all you're ensuring is that people only like you because you're easy to be around. Because you go with the flow. Because you don't do anything that might cause others to actually *feel* something. But then no one knows who you really are. So yes, maybe people won't be intimidated or threatened by you, but they also won't be challenged, inspired, excited, or intrigued by you either. When you don't dull your true essence, but embody it instead, you create an opportunity for others to love the person that you are. Be liked by all and be loved by few, or be loved by those who matter and not liked by those who don't. The choice is yours.

They say I have to pick a voice
As if it's just a simple choice
They scream over one another
One thought alone pulling me under
Both whispering that they're my friend
And that if I just listen to them, then in the end
Everything will be as it should
So why do I feel so misunderstood?
One of them is after me
While the other wants me to break free
Can't quiet the constant bickering in my head
Between ED vs. ED

The Truth Teller, written in 2007 in treatment for my Eating Disorder

CHAPTER 9

THE TRUTH ABOUT
RESTRICTION

"I remember a time when I made myself small because others found me intimidating. I figured if I could just play small others would feel more comfortable. But that time is long gone."
— Maryam Hasnaa (@maryamhasnaa)

So, remember in the preface of this book I told you that there was time when I didn't embody my full self? Yeah, this is the chapter about that. It's about the period in my life where I started to shrink myself so that other people could more easily digest me. So that I didn't have to feel the weight of other people's shame. It was the time I turned on myself and became my own worst enemy so that I could hurt myself before anyone else could hurt me. It was the time I lost sight of my inner truth completely. So, without further ado, let's dive in.

As you can probably gather by now, I am confident, bold, articulate, and don't take any shit from anyone. This is my true nature. If you were ever to have the pleasure of watching any of the classic Demar home-videos, you would see that not a segment goes by where I'm not jumping in front of the camera trying to get my Dad to film me dance or asking him if we could watch the video right after (yes, because I thought I was entertaining and loved looking at myself on the screen). And, to illustrate the point even further, let me tell you about the time my mom took me to work for "bring your daughter to work day". I was eight years old. My mom, being a woman in business who is high up in the ranks, would at times experience moments at work when she wasn't always treated with the respect she deserved. And, as her daughter, I'd overheard her, at home, talking about these situations on various occasions. So, here I am, my little pee-wee self with pigtails in, standing beside her as she introduced me to a tall man in a suit. And, very loudly and proudly, I looked up at the man and asked, "Are you the one who is being mean to my mommy?" Now, I later found out that this was *not* the same man who was, in fact, mean to my mommy. But the point was that, even at the ripe young age of eight, I was not going to allow any BS to slide. That was my inner truth. And I was going to speak the truth, no matter what, if it meant standing up for who or what needed to be stood up for.

So, being such an outspoken, direct individual who takes no shit means I play on *a lot* of people's insecurities. It's not by choice, or on purpose, but it is the reality. People get triggered by those who say that thing that shakes up the vibe of the room. And being made to feel like you're "too much" or "too intense" or "too outspoken" for many years would make anyone feel the need to tone it down just to survive in our crazy world. Such was the case with me. I was always a naturally small girl, so when I started to restrict my intake, it didn't take long for me to be in the "danger zone" weight-wise. I was in high school when I went to my annual doctor's appointment and was diagnosed with anorexia nervosa.

At the time, I didn't know what eating disorders were, as we'd never gotten that education in school (which is another serious issue, altogether). Like many young people my age, I thought that people with eating disorders hated themselves, hated their bodies, and hated their lives. (Social media hadn't yet blown up at the time, so I wasn't hearing any stories about people my age struggling with similar issues. And there weren't many accurate depictions of eating disorders in movies or television, either.) But I didn't hate myself, my body, or my life. Like I said, I was confident. I wasn't someone who had ever previously dieted or been concerned with my appearance in the slightest. My family members had a healthy relationship with food. Our snack drawers were always fully stocked. We weren't deprived or told we shouldn't eat certain things. And I didn't have some "big life crisis" that I associated with anyone having something as serious as an eating disorder. All I knew was that, suddenly, I was concerned with every morsel of food that entered my body (or, frankly, that didn't). On the surface, that is.

The truth is—eating disorders are not about food. At all. Food, or a lack thereof, is used as a mechanism through which to cope.

On the outside, it didn't appear that I had much to cope with in any traumatic sense. I was sixteen years old, young and vivacious, had many friends, a boyfriend, made straight A's (including in AP classes), danced multiple times a week and was in the front row of every recital, was auditioning for acting jobs through my agent (which soon led to my role on Gossip Girl), and lived in a well-to-do neighborhood with a happy, healthy family—the list goes on. What was traumatic about that? Well, I was terrified of growing up. I wanted a way to numb myself and not feel all of the many deep, intense feelings I often had. I didn't want to have to care as much as I did about relationships that seemed to always lack the same amount of care from the other side. I wanted protection and safety from people that had hurt me emotionally. I wanted a way to separate myself from others and have a unique identity that no one could take away from me. I wanted something to make me feel a sense of power and control. All of this was subconscious, of course. All of this was uncovered over the course of my treatment. I won't get into all the many layers and causal factors of the disorder, as that would be a whole other book, but what I will say is this: eating disorders are layered, complex disorders that are over-simplified, mocked, and even glorified in our image-obsessed culture. It is no longer cool, and it never was, to say that you wish you had an eating disorder. It just shows how out of touch you are.

Eating disorders are the *opposite* of glamorous. They destroy your body and your life and kill you slowly but surely. You will never be able to live a full life on an empty stomach. You don't "want" to be anorexic. The only people who say they wish they had an eating disorder are those who know nothing about the reality of them, or who incorrectly believe that having the deadly disorder will somehow make their lives better. *How sad is that?* Here's some of the nightmarish reality of eating disorders: no energy; no excitement; consistent thoughts of food and weight and calories; intense fear of gaining weight; lack of interest in things you previously loved; distanced relationships with all those around you; weigh-ins; treatment centers; tears; anguish; despair; physical and emotional pain; and more. So, no, you don't *wish* you had an eating disorder. It's like saying you wish you had a terminal illness. Anorexia nervosa has one of the highest mortality rates of any mental illness. I'm one of the lucky ones who survived and made it through to help others on their own journeys to recovery. Many don't make it.

More and more of our young people are developing eating disorders at an increasing rate. Of course, we can talk about the social media factor, which absolutely plays a role. (Is it the sole cause? Certainly not. I didn't have any form of social media until well into my recovery.) But what we also need to consider, societally, are the messages that we give to people. That they are "too much" (or, conversely, that they are "not enough.") We need to stop making people feel as if they need to tone it down in some way to appease others. All of these messages tell us that we're the problem and that we need to do something about it, even if that means starving ourselves to death. Consider the impact the next time you take out your invisible tape measure and try and tell someone how much of this or that they ought to be in comparison to what they naturally are. Now, I'm not saying that someone calling you "too much" or "not enough" is the sole cause of an eating disorder. Like I said, there is no one sole cause. But these messages certainly *can be* a contributing underlying factor to why someone feels the need to make themselves disappear.

We need to develop more awareness and compassion around mental illness. Because, let me tell you something: I will never forget the older girls in the high school cafeteria laughing at me and yelling at me to eat something from the next table over while all those around gawked and whispered. I won't forget the time when someone who I thought was my best friend commented on a Facebook photo of me saying I looked like a Holocaust survivor. I won't forget the stares and the mockery and how utterly alone and isolated I felt as I battled my disorder. And I know that none of that was a reflection of me, but of other people's true colors and society's lack of understanding and awareness of mental health. It's an ugly quality of our society that no one should be proud of in the slightest.

It was only in my recovery (beginning the summer before college) that I began to learn that I was never the problem. Society was. The messages I received from others was. The lack of education about mental health was. I wasn't. I was, in fact, exactly how I was supposed to be. I was just struggling, like we all do at some point in our lives. And for me, that struggle took the form of an eating disorder. And, truthfully, I thank my lucky stars all the time that I had that life-wrenching struggle early on in my life. Because, now that I've worked through that and recovered, I've already invested a great deal of time into working on myself. Of course, I'm always continuing to learn and grow, because I value self-work and believe it's a life-long process for every human being. But my inner vulnerabilities are not a mystery to me, because I've identified them and I have the tools to work through them. If I hadn't faced my eating disorder head on, I'd never be where I currently am. You will never, ever regret putting in the work, but you will absolutely regret it if you don't.

And in my growth, I revisited my younger self for answers. Because, before society got to me, I had my truth. I lived it. I wasn't afraid or ashamed of my inherent power. I went back and visited that little girl with the pigtails who stood triumphantly next to my mom to tell off the person whom I thought had made her feel badly. She did not deserve to be toned down. She deserved to have her voice heard. She deserved to have her presence known and felt, in full. And I can't tell you how drastically my life has improved since I came back to that inner child and released the burden of other people's shame and fear they projected onto me and that I'd subsequently internalized.

It was never mine to begin with, and it's not yours, either. I recovered not because of anyone yelling at me to eat something. I recovered not because my "friend" commented on my Facebook post that I looked like a Holocaust survivor. I recovered not because of the stares and the ridicule I faced. I recovered *in spite* of all of that. And you can recover from whatever it is you might be struggling with, too. It requires you to get quiet, sit still, and do that introspective work. It requires you to look at your own reflection, call that inner child to mind, and start sorting through what is your own truth and what is simply a projection from those around you.

For me, recovery looked like long walks around my neighborhood. I'd spend time in nature, listening to its beautiful symphony, and allowing my own thoughts and feelings to fill the space. Recovery looked like a lot of journaling, including poetry and letters I'd write between myself and the eating disorder. (Those who've been to treatment for an eating disorder know that we refer to the voice of the eating disorder as "ED." Well, my initials are also "ED." So I'd write about the battle between "ED vs. ED" and how I was going to allow the healthy "ED" to win out in the end.) Recovery for me looked like confronting my triggers as they came up. It looked like reframing negative thought patterns. It looked like a lot of encouraging self-talk. It looked like a series of moments in which I gave myself permission, over and over again, to do what I knew fundamentally was the right thing for myself and my body in the long run. My recovery looked like speaking my truth instead of swallowing it in order to avoid potential conflict. My recovery looked like coming back to my inner child and letting her know that she was never "too much" and that she was just the right amount, all along.

We all have ways in which we restrict ourselves. It may not take the form of an eating disorder, but there are many ways in which we shrink ourselves to become more digestible for those around us. Or, even, to become more digestible to ourselves. We internalize the messages we receive from our loved ones and society on a subconscious level, and these internalized messages become our own limiting beliefs. That is, unless we consciously do the work to reframe them. What have you been told about yourself that has become part of your subconscious narrative? What beliefs are you still holding onto about yourself that may be untrue or outdated? This may not be obvious at first glance. But you can find the answers in how you speak to yourself. Are there things you continually repeat about yourself that have become part of your working narrative? Things you tell yourself you can do and things that you cannot? Where do these thoughts stem from? Usually, they don't originate from you yourself. This is where the inner work comes in. Begin to explore how the things you've been told about yourself or the ways in which you've been treated have formed your own self-image. Then, you can begin to separate out what you actually believe to be true and what has just become a part of your story based on an outdated tale that no longer resonates with you. Or perhaps it never really resonated with you at all.

This is where you give yourself permission. Permission to let go of what doesn't belong to you. Permission to release what doesn't resonate. Permission to pick up that metaphorical pen and re-write your narrative in a way that adequately reflects who you are. Not who you once were. Not who you've been told you are. Not what your limiting beliefs tell you you are. Give yourself permission be the author of your own story. We're all the experts on ourselves, at the end of the day. So

RESTRICTION

when someone comes to you with their imaginary measuring tape, give yourself permission to ignore it and come back to the truth of who you are. Which, my friend, has always been enough.

They told her to just start
But starting was the hardest part
She knew it in her heart
You can't rush art

Yet perhaps she clung
Too tightly on this rung
Of patience that she sung
Limiting beliefs on the tip of her tongue

Yes, of course it takes time
And while all of that is fine
Maybe there was another line
Of truth keeping her behind

So she sat still and she listened
To her actual intuition
Which told her that her vision
Was on the other side of her permission.

The Truth Teller

CHAPTER 10

THE TRUTH ABOUT
PERMISSION

*"Don't look for society to give you
permission to be yourself."*
— *Steve Maraboli*

'd venture to say that most of us are waiting on some kind
of permission. Maybe it's permission to tell someone you're
interested in how you really feel about them. Maybe it's
permission to take more time out of your week for self-care.
Perhaps it's permission to take a step back from a friendship
that is no longer serving you. We feel we need permission from
others for a variety of reasons. We're conditioned to believe it's
"selfish" to go after our personal goals. We're given the message that we shouldn't speak unless we're asked for our opinion. We're taught to take up less space and not ask for more of
it. So we're operating from this false premise that any action
we want to take needs approval from others before going after
it. And that is why so many dreams are slept on and so many
lives are lived for those around them rather than for the person
themselves.

**It's not just because we're waiting on permis-
sion from others, it's also because we don't
realize the permission that matters most is
our own.**

The idea that the only permission we *truly* need comes from
within is a novel concept to many of us, although it shouldn't
be. We've all been in situations where we've been given that

permission by others, but it still isn't enough to get the ball rolling on actual change. And that's because we haven't given ourselves the green light. We haven't made a conscious choice, so we hold ourselves back. Deep down, we know we're the only ones who can actually propel our dreams into motion. But our second-guessing and overwhelming fears often paralyze us before anything gets done.

I had to give myself permission to write this book. It was a dream I'd had for a very long time. I used to sit at the kitchen table with my Bubbie, my mother's mother (who sadly passed away in September of 2022, but I got the chance to tell her that I'd written this book and that it's dedicated to her). Bubbie was, and still is, one of my best friends in the entire world. She'd babysit my brother and me when my parents took the occasional vacation just the two of them. Bubbie and I would sit at the kitchen table and write chapter books and poetry and she'd always tell me, "Emma, you have a gift. You have a way with words. It's really something. I know you are going to be an author." Since Bubbie was one of the few people that knew me deeply, from the inside out, when she told me something about myself, I always took it to heart. I thought back to her words often as I wrote this book.

And although my Bubbie's words helped give me that extra encouragement to write, it would not have been enough on its own if I did not also permit myself to go for it. Because, ultimately, no matter how many creative writing professors I had or how many family members or friends complimented my writing skills, I still could've slept on my words. And there were numerous excuses I could've granted myself for not going after this dream of mine. Everyone has an opinion, and I knew putting myself out there would open me up to potential criticism. I'm a perfectionist when it comes to my creativity, and what if I couldn't live up to what I knew intrinsically I was capable of? What if I was in over my head? All of these thoughts could have thwarted me from just diving in. But I gave myself permission *in spite* of all that.

How? By being connected to my inner truth. The truth that made itself evident every time I put pen to paper. The fact that my fingers would come alive on the keyboard and dance across the concepts effortlessly. The fact that I was able to weave alliteration and symbols throughout extended metaphors naturally. The fact that, whenever I was going through something challenging in my life, I turned to writing. Or that whenever I needed to make sense of something, I'd reflect on it through journaling. Writing has been a constant throughout every chapter of my life. It's how I come back to myself. And yes, of course the words from my loved ones, like Bubbie, gave me that extra boost of assurance as I embarked on the journey of writing this book. But without a conscious decision on my part to really go for it—it would have never happened.

The thing is, in order to give yourself permission for whatever it is you want to do, you're going to have to give people back their projections. Because, oftentimes, it's these projections that stop us right in our tracks. They give us pause. They become our own limiting beliefs. And, sometimes, it's not even that someone has directly said something to you, but that you're *imagining* they might. As I wrote this book, I was fully aware of what some might say about it. "Wow, who does she think she is writing a book? Why does she think anyone actually *cares* about what she has to say?" Naturally, many people would allow these types of thoughts to dissuade them from continuing on. But I knew those thoughts did not belong to me. I knew they were fears that stemmed from hearing people judge others for putting their own personal work out there in the world (usually spoken by those who would never dare to be brave enough, themselves). It is only those who don't have the self-confidence and courage to pursue their own passions who will judge you for pursuing yours. So you need to come back to your truth. For me, I know exactly why I'm writing this. I know how much work has gone into it. I know where I am coming from with the words I put out there, and I'm fully confident in them. I know that it takes creativity, insight, wisdom, dedication, courage, consistency, and a lot fucking more to write a whole ass book. And guess what it takes to sit back and judge? Nothing. There you go. I gave myself permission.

Anyone can tell you that you're allowed to go after your dreams. But if you still hold yourself back because you don't think your voice matters or you're afraid of what others might think, then you won't sustain any real progress on whatever it is you're working on. You will abandon ship whenever you have a moment of doubt or experience an ounce of criticism from the outside world. The permission you need to give yourself is that, in spite of your limiting beliefs, and in spite of naysayers and skeptics, you know you deserve to pursue your purpose. No one has the power to prevent you from doing so. You are the one who is with yourself at the end of the day when your head hits the pillow. It is your job to grant yourself permission to do what will make you proud.

I could have waited endlessly on permission. It would have been the safer option, for sure. I'd never have to face the fear and vulnerability of putting myself out there and the uncertainty of how it'll be received. I could have let this book live inside me forever and could continue to stay quiet about the things that matter most to me. I could dull myself down to make others more comfortable. But as soon as I realized that everything I wanted was on the other side of my own permission slip, I finally allowed myself to live in my full expression. And for me, living as my full self means being bold and existing loudly. It means not apologizing for taking up space or for saying things that could potentially rub others the wrong way. It's scary to give yourself permission to go after your goals. To be all that you are without apologizing for it. If it wasn't scary, we'd all be doing it.

So, how do we give ourselves permission? To give myself permission, I had to go back to my inner child, of course. Our inner children know who we are, fundamentally. They hold the wisdom of our truth. We need to unlearn all of these toxic messages from society that make us inhibited and question ourselves. I thought about my inner child and the kind of life that she wanted and deserved. She always lived fully. She didn't hold back. And that girl still lives inside of me. She is me and I am her. She deserves to be heard and to be seen. She speaks my truth. And I give myself permission to do what is in her best interests. Because any other way I've tried to live here on earth, aside from being my full self, has never made me happy. And until I really listened to her, I was never going to feel fully myself. The same goes for you and your inner child.

So I have this continual inner dialogue with my inner child. Yes, the one with the pigtails. She helps to guide me through my life. I ask her how she'd feel if I never wrote that book she always dreamed about. She told me very loudly and clearly that if I didn't write it, she'd make sure that I'd regret it forever. Ha! Love her sass. What's your inner child like? What would she/he/they say if you told them you weren't going to pursue that dream they always had their hearts set on? What would they say if you told them you lived your life holding yourself back for fear of taking up too much space? Have these conversations and have them often. Your inner child knows you better than any of those friends or family members who you routinely turn to for the answers.

Giving yourself permission means you value yourself enough to go after the vision you have for your life. It means you know that you're the conductor of your existence and that you'll never accomplish what you want to unless you go after it whole heartedly. It means you're connected to your truth and are determined to live in line with that truth. And, many times, you have to give yourself permission *in spite* of your fears, insecurities, and potential scrutiny from others. You're letting yourself know that *even though* people might not understand what you're doing, that you *still* honor yourself enough to go after the life you know is meant for you. That you know you deserve to live out your truth, in full.

If you're waiting on permission from others, you'll be waiting forever. Because you're looking in the wrong place. Even if someone does give you permission, it will never feel like enough until you give it to yourself. So, look within. Find that inner child of yours that is buried beneath the cobwebs of lies, hypocrisy and judgements from the outside. Stop waiting on permission slips from people who don't know how to give their own selves permission. Ask your inner child what she is waiting for permission on. Listen to her. Respect her. Love her. And grant her permission.

Standing there on the brink
Of despair, the icy cold air
Sashaying through my hair
Whispering secrets into my ears
As the words begin to form a coat
Layering the walls of my throat
My mouth agape so out they float
For they so urgently need to be spoke

And there they all sit
Grinning as they tap their fingertips
Deadpan expressions, unmoving lips
Their masks of care, carefully slicked
Expressions as barren as the sticks
Of branches as the clock ticks
And my words begin to stiffen, quick
They've been falling into a baren ditch
For their response I can already predict.

The Truth Teller

CHAPTER 11

THE TRUTH ABOUT
COMMUNICATION

"Talking isn't the same as connecting.
Connecting has energy and flow behind it. Rivers
beneath the surface of what is heard."
— *Victoria Erickson*

Have you ever tried to express your feelings to someone and they've made it seem like you're creating conflict? Have you been labeled "aggressive" when you're simply angry and trying to communicate that anger? Or do you know people who, anytime you bring something up that is the slightest bit controversial, cringe awkwardly or become combative? Or they make you feel wrong for bringing up anything that isn't "positive" or agreeable? If anything of the sort has ever happened to you, which I'm sure it has, this chapter is for you. Why am I sure it has? Because we live in a society that has incredibly poor communication skills, and therefore does not know how to handle healthy communication. Moreover, our society often confuses being direct and straightforward with creating conflict. And news flash: they are not the same.

One of the main reasons our communication has suffered greatly over the past few decades is, of course, technology. We've replaced good ol' heart-to-hearts with text exchanges. We've replaced showing others how we feel *on our actual faces* with emojis. Hand-written letters? We left them in the 90's. We've forgotten how to communicate. We aren't practicing the art of comprehension and active listening. So, when someone *does* come along and shares how they feel, we often don't know how to receive it. We're suspicious of their motivations. And, on top of that, we often don't even *want* to engage, because then we might get pulled into the communication part, which we are trying desperately to avoid. When we engage, we must confront what's underneath the surface, which is usually exactly what we're afraid of.

Oftentimes it's fear that prevents someone from saying how they feel, or from actively listening to someone else express their feelings. Maybe you didn't come from a family where you talked about your feelings. And, listen, that's not your *fault*. But it's important to be *conscious* of it so that you're aware that this is an area you need to work on. Or maybe you haven't yet given yourself *permission* to communicate how you feel because you don't think your feelings are valid. Or maybe you're traumatized from a time where you *did* work up the courage to say what was in your heart and it didn't go well. And it's understandable, and valid, that you wouldn't want to go down that road again. But shutting down completely isn't the answer, either. We need to find a way to get back on the communication train instead of going to the other extreme and not expressing ourselves at all.

The thing is that, when we communicate, we cannot control others' reactions to what we say. We can only control what comes out of our own mouths. And this can be scary. We might pour our heart out to someone only for them to barely bat an eyelid. So, we need to be aware of this, going into any sort of conversation. What we need to do is let go of outcomes that we cannot control. So, some may be asking, well then what's the point of communicating if no one is going to understand? Well, the purpose of communication isn't always to make the other person change or to see it from your perspective. And, in fact, it shouldn't be. You'll waste your precious time and energy if your goal is to try and prove yourself, and your opinions, to others. A great goal in communicating, though, is to honor how you feel by allowing yourself to express your true emotions. Again, if we go back to that inner child of ours, we want to allow their voice to be heard. Otherwise, they will throw a tantrum, and this tantrum may come out passive-aggressively. And that's never effective.

I'm a firm believer in allowing my truth to exist out there in the world. Many times this has served me well. And, in the past, there were times that it's caused conflict. But sometimes conflict is necessary in order to promote healthy change. Either way, I've learned over time how to make my inner truth heard in an effective way. The only way to learn healthy communication is to practice it. And in our society, we often get the message to just let things go. We're told it isn't "cool" to explain ourselves. But maybe it's just avoidance. Maybe it's fear talking. Maybe we're erring too far on the side of extreme caution when it comes to vocalizing our truth. Perhaps it's time to bring our truths to light.

And, if and when you do express yourself, and you're not met with understanding, here are a few things to remember: It's usually not about you. When someone is refusing to hear you out, it's often because they don't want to. They're not interested in hearing what you have to say. Or maybe they just don't want to have to deal with it. Or maybe they're incapable because they haven't learned how to communicate themselves. But wouldn't you rather know this? I mean, if not, you need to question why you don't value being understood in your relationships, or why it isn't important to you to be in relationships with others that are emotionally compatible with you. If you avoid relationships where feelings are spoken about, this might stem from a fear of getting close to others or having them see the real you. So what mask are you wearing here? If you really want to determine the nature of your relationships, you must bring your full self to the table. Otherwise, there is no real connection there. You're just co-existing.

Being on "good terms" with someone isn't the same thing as having a real connection with them.

You can be on "good terms" with a lot of people and none of those people might feel truly connected to you. I certainly know a few people in my life who operate this way. They may have a lot of friends, but the amount of effort they put forth into these relationships is minimal. Especially on the communication front. And friends who talk about the weather and television shows aren't the same types of friends who know one another's dreams, passions, fears or even darkest traumas. And, yes, there is space for all kinds of friendships. There's nothing wrong with having friendships where you talk about more concrete concepts, like a shared interest or profession. But if *all* your friendships exist on this wavelength, that's something to think about. Why is this? Being "good" with someone is easy. You show up when you're supposed to. You say the "right things." You do what is apropos. You can do all of this without revealing any truth about yourself. But having a real *connection* requires depth. It requires truly knowing and connecting with that other person. It requires a certain warmth and understanding. It requires a recognition of the soul within the other. It requires healthy communication.

So, let's be clear here: Communication does not *equal* conflict. Just because someone wants to share how they feel with you or has an alternative viewpoint doesn't mean they're out to get you. (And if you think this way, perhaps you ought to look at where this paranoia is stemming from). We need to remember that communication is *necessary*. It's important. It helps people feel connected and brings them closer together. It helps us to avoid making assumptions about how someone feels. It helps us to avoid behaving in passive-aggressive ways that often cause way more problems than direct communication can. Direct communication asks you to be fully present with another person. It forces you to show up, hold space, and be patient. (Patience? In the day and age of everything being right at our fingertips? Yes, patience is still a thing.) People who are afraid of communication often label it as something "negative" or "unnecessary." And by placing these unfavorable labels onto it, they're both giving themselves permission to avoid the communication and making you feel bad for being direct. We need healthy communication if we want to have healthy relationships. And, yes, communication *can* involve conflict. But you know what *certainly* brings conflict? Lack of communication. You can guarantee that there will be conflict when you don't say how you feel or don't listen to someone else's feelings. That's a sure way to create a real issue.

When you avoid speaking about the things that are necessary to talk about, you can be sure that conflict will fall right into your lap. And it will not look as pretty as healthy communication does. It might include outbursts of anger and pain that has been stored up for lack of being expressed. It might eat away at you and cause distance both with yourself and others. Avoiding communicating your feelings will do that. And if what you're looking for is peace, you won't find it by not communicating. Communication has the power to *resolve* conflict. Even if there's conflict initially within the communication, if two parties are active participants in the conversation, then you have an opportunity to move through it and to come to some sort of resolution. But avoiding communication? That will guarantee that you will be surrounded by conflict, both internally and externally. And who wants that?

Look, you can choose to plug your ears and not listen to the feelings of others. You can avoid saying how you feel. You can run from communication as fast as you want to. But just know that doing so will not bring you tranquility. It's not going to help resolve conflict. It's not going to make your inner child feel heard. The people around you probably won't feel very connected to you. Your relationships will suffer. You will be alone with your feelings until the end of time. I mean, hey, you can go for it! But why the heck would you?

"Just go with the flow!" They chanted
Like they're imparting some novel wisdom
Waving their copycat flags around in unison
Not understanding why I don't want to join in

But their flow is littered with the debris
Of other people's limiting beliefs
And the hidden agendas that they don't see
They parade around as though they are free

As they listen for directions on how to move
Just to fit into someone else's groove
I watch them stumble upon one another's toes
While I follow my own flow.

The Truth Teller

CHAPTER 12

THE TRUTH ABOUT
GOING WITH
THE FLOW

"The 'belonging' gained from following the crowd is not belonging. It is performative self-abandonment."
—Shannon Kaiser (@shannonkaiserwrites)

Remember when we talked about the "I'm a good guy" mask? Yeah, it's time to elaborate on that. You know those people who love to tell you how easygoing they are? It's always one of the first things they'll tell you about themselves. It's seen as a bragging right—"I'm so cool that I can just flow with anything." *Um... is that really cool?* Or, "I'm such a 'nice' person because I just go with the flow." Why is being agreeable and accommodating instead of stating your real opinions, which may not be so agreeable, personality traits to strive for? Well, maybe there is a reason that so many people from all walks of life use this catchall empty phrase to describe their personality. It's because many are afraid. Going with the flow keeps you safe, after all. Also, it's easy.

Because when you go with the flow, you don't have to find your *own* flow.

There were many instances in my past, before I learned to follow my own flow, that I followed the flow of others and it wound up biting me in the ass. Like the time in high school, when I decided to follow the flow of my friends who were drinking in a public park—I didn't even drink at the time. So I decided to just shut up about it, even though I was anxious about getting into trouble. The cops showed up and took us all down to the station (not to arrest anyone but to scare us). My dad had to rescue me from the police station. Luckily, my parents both knew I wasn't engaging in anything aside from going with the flow and joining my friends while they drank in a park. I was also anorexic at the time and was afraid to drink for a variety of reasons. But the cops in our town were bored so they'd busy themselves with scare tactics. Or the time where my friend convinced me to leave art class early when we had a substitute and I ended up getting the first and only detention I've ever had. Basically, any and every time I've ignored my instincts to follow the flow of others, there've been repercussions that were never pleasant or characteristic of me as a person. It's never made me feel good to go with the flow of the crowd, especially when I knew better.

If you're consistently going *with* the flow, then you're undoubtedly neglecting your *own* flow, which includes your voice and needs. There is no possible way you're happy or okay with *every single thing* ever brought to your attention, so you're lying to yourself and others when you act like you don't care either way about anything. You *do* care. You *do* have an opinion. You're just not stating it. And why aren't you stating it? Well, you're afraid. Standing up and stating your opinion, especially when it differs from the crowd's consensus, requires true courage. I obviously didn't want to be the only one who wasn't going to the park with my high school friends. And I didn't want to be the straight lace who wouldn't leave class a few minutes early because she was too scared of the repercussions. It takes vulnerability to stand apart from the crowd. It takes courage to make your needs and opinions known. Because when you go with your own flow, you risk others not agreeing with that flow. You risk disconnection from those who don't accept you taking an alternative route on your roadmap. So, in order not to face that potential shame and scrutiny, people disappear into the flow of others.

You can't follow your flow if you don't trust the source of that flow. In other words, if you don't trust your intuition and what it says to you, then you're not going to feel comfortable listening to it. Many people who don't follow their own flow look toward others because they don't trust their internal sense of guidance. They look toward a group, or a strong authority figure, to present to them the "right" way to be. They don't need to think for themselves, or to come up with their own moral compass to live by, because it's all laid out for them. Then, if things don't turn out the way that they hope, they don't have to blame themselves. They blame whatever or whomever they are following. They don't need to take real accountability for their actions, because they don't see themselves as part of the problem. They've exempted themselves from the whole discussion. And then they wonder why they continue to spiral through the same experiences over and over again. Well, if you don't trust yourself enough to take risks and do the internal reflection when things don't turn out like you want them to, in order to see what you can adjust next time around, you'll never move forward. You'll never have the courage to go your own way, even if going your own way may be the best thing you can do for yourself.

Before I hear the "well, going with the flow is just being a good person" rationale (which is really said to make you feel better about following the flow and to encourage those around you to do the same), let me say this: you can be a good person while *not* always going with the flow. Furthermore, you're not necessarily a good person just *because* you go with the flow.

You can be a good person *and* still stand up for what you believe in even if others disagree and decide not to like you for it. And when you stand up for what you believe in and you lead with honesty and integrity, *that's* true kindness. You are also setting an example of being true to yourself. Others may not like it (especially if your opinion differs from their own or if they don't benefit from it in some way), but that doesn't equal "being mean." In fact, what is truly kind is to follow your own intuition because that means you're being sincere.

Let's talk about when it *is* appropriate to go with the flow, because I know there will be those of you out there reading this who are waving their flags of disapproval. When you're at work, for example, there are certain rules and regulations you must follow. There's a certain professional flow that you're expected to abide by, and yes, you ought to follow it if you want to keep your job. But even in this instance, hopefully, by following this flow you're not compromising your character or personal values. You're just playing a role based on a part of your life that requires such a role to function. Or, if you're at a doctor's appointment, you're going to have to follow proper protocol to be helped. So, yes, there are certain instances in life when we must go with the flow. It would be complete anarchy for everyone to just do whatever the fuck they want in any instance and never follow any societal rules and regulations. But the *real* flow you should always be following is that which is in alignment with your true nature and doing what is ultimately in your best interests. And acting out when it's inappropriate or going against the grain just to create a ruckus doesn't count as following your own flow. That behavior is just plain obnoxious.

Going with the flow is avoiding real life. Life is going to have obstacles. You're going to have conflict, whether you like it or not. The *only* way to go through life without conflict is to avoid it. And why are you avoiding it? Well, most likely because you don't want to deal with it, which is why we tend to avoid things. Why don't you want to deal with it? Because conflict isn't "fun." Because having to express our needs in front of others (especially people who we know might not agree) can feel very scary. So we run away from that feeling at all costs. We act like we agree when we don't. We don't state our needs. We silence ourselves. We dull down our uniqueness. We distance ourselves from our anxiety by avoiding the cause. By avoiding reality.

Reality is, you don't agree with everyone. Reality is, *you* don't like everyone. So why are you acting like you do? Listen, I'm not recommending to be a jerk. I'm just saying quit *pretending*. Be honest when you have a different feeling than your friend. Don't be scared to disagree when the crowd says something you can't stand behind. Don't dull yourself down and become a contortionist just to keep the peace. The truth is that by avoiding uncomfortable feelings in the short term, you're setting yourself up for a waterfall of them later in life. You'll realize that you've lived your life running away from yourself. That you've lived your life in shallow, dead-end, or even toxic relationships because you were too scared to walk away. That you lived your life out of fear and avoidance. That you're sleepwalking through your life.

We love to shame others for not going with the flow. We tell them to be more agreeable and to just "get over it" and "be the bigger person." We make them feel selfish for having needs. We make them feel crazy for stating their differing opinions. Going with the flow is not always good advice, and we need to stop acting as though it is. Many times, when people tell you to go with the flow, it's because they don't want to deal with your unique perspective. They want to shut you up. They want to quiet you. Going with the flow might mean not speaking up about something you should *absolutely* speak up about. In actuality, much of the time "going with the flow" is poor advice and can cause you a lot of personal damage.

When I've been told to go with the flow, it's always in response to me having differing opinions or desires from those around me. It's meant to quiet my inner truth and to get me to shut up and keep the peace. And perhaps there's a time and place for that, but it's definitely not a motto to live by. Because what it tells us is to silence our inner voice—our inner knowing—and that what's going on around us takes precedence over what's within. It discourages us from trusting ourselves and our intuition. And trusting ourselves is the basis of confidence. It gives us the message that in order to survive in this world, we need to dull ourselves and look externally for the direction we should take. Is that the message we want to be spreading?

Oftentimes, the people who want you to go with their flow believe their flow is the *only* flow. In other words, they believe their way is the right way. So, it's not just that they're wanting you to be accommodating, but they don't believe there's any alternative route worth taking. There've been many times in my life where I've watched the shock on people's faces when they realize I took my own route and wound up exactly where I said I'd be. For example, in building my social media presence as That Trendy Therapist™, I was faced with many different opinions about what I should or shouldn't put out there. There were people, who of course weren't even therapists themselves, who told me that what I was posting wouldn't be helpful to potential clients. But as I continued to go my own way and trust my internal sense of guidance, as I always do, I watched my account steadily rise and gain traction. I continued to get more and more of those daily messages about how I was helping people find the courage to use their voice and how my account is the *only* thing that made them feel deeply understood. Imagine if I'd listened to those who had given me that unsolicited advice? What a tragedy that would've been.

Don't let the wind blow you through life. Your life will have little meaning (to you or to anyone else) if you do. Don't be afraid to give a fuck. Yes, it takes an abundance of courage to have an opinion and to state your needs. It can be scary if you've spent your life never showing your full deck. But if you're living your whole life going with the flow, know that you may be living your life out of fear. Understand that you're probably acting out of avoidance. Consider that you might be setting yourself up for more pain in the long run. What you don't deal with now will run your life later on. And then, you won't be able to just "go with the flow," because you'll be stuck dealing with all of those things you've pushed down *in order to* go with that flow.

See, here's the truth about people who "go with the flow." They're not going with their *own* flow. They're going with the flow of *others*. The flow of life shouldn't be blindly operated by an outside source. It should come from within you. Live with intention. It begins with that inner wisdom and gut feeling that so many people are out of touch with. And you continue to lose touch with your inner knowing when you're constantly looking outside of yourself for a sense of guidance. If you're honest, you're not going with the flow because you're a "nice person," you're going with the flow because you're scared, you don't trust yourself, and it's easier to follow others. Sorry, I'm not sorry. It must be said. Stop fooling yourself into thinking you're some "zen" creature who has never thought a thought that differed from that of the crowd. While you may think you come off as easygoing, those who are perceptive might see you as fake, passive, or ingenuous. And that's the truth. Find your flow.

No, it's not that she's dramatic
Or erratic or aristocratic or problematic
But they toss around these labels
From across the dinner table

After receiving a set of boundaries
Ones they should've seen coming
While they get lost in the scapegoating
Convincing themselves their hands are clean

They would prefer to make that the narrative
So that they can read themselves their delusional
Fairytales to help them fall asleep
But they lie awake while she sleeps in utter peace.

The Truth Teller

CHAPTER 13

THE TRUTH ABOUT
BOUNDARIES

"When you start setting boundaries, some relationships will fall apart because you disregarding yourself was what held them together."
— *Annalie Howling (@annaliehowling)*

In order to go with your own flow, you need to set boundaries. Ah, good ol' boundaries. You've heard about them. Maybe you've established some with angry in-laws or ex-partners. Maybe you've had them created for you (probably not to your liking). Few people like to be on the receiving end of boundaries, so let's start there. Because before I talk about how essential boundaries are and that we can't live our healthiest lives without them, we need to get real about the fact that they're not always pleasant. It can be painful when a loved one sets a boundary with us. And it can be painful to create that boundary, as well. But neither of those statements means that boundaries aren't essential to establish.

The reason we need boundaries is to protect our space, time, and energy. We need boundaries so that we have enough room to feel our own feelings without being trampled on by those of others. We need boundaries to protect our hard-earned energy, the natural energy inside us that we work so hard to generate. We need boundaries to manage our time so that our life is our own and works for us. We need boundaries to protect ourselves from the toxicity of others. We all need boundaries. We all must set boundaries. But most often, when we set them, we get backlash from people who benefited from us having none.

Of course, someone who had a key to your house might be upset when you take it away. You're taking away their *access* to you. People like having access to other people for a variety of reasons. They may feel in control of you if they have free reign of where and when they see you. They may get their sense of self-worth through their relationship with you, so any way that you block their ability to spend time with you is intolerable to them. But whatever the situation, here's the point: the only people who are calling you "mean" for setting boundaries with them are those who are upset because they don't want you to have them. Their reaction to your boundaries says little about the boundaries themselves and a lot about the nature of the relationship itself.

There was a time I had to create boundaries around certain people who proved to be toxic to my mental health. Unfortunately, these individuals showed time and again that they didn't have my best interests at heart. This was made clear, over time, through passive-aggressive statements and their resistance to listening, and truly considering, anything I had to say. Of course, when I started setting boundaries, I got pushback. I was called a lot of names. The guilt tripping was endless. What they were missing was that this was not a "battle of wills" that I would just drop once I stopped being "stubborn," but a conscious effort to set boundaries based on real life events. To them, I was just being "rude" and holding a grudge.

There's a difference between holding a grudge and creating a necessary boundary. People who consider it a grudge are refusing to look at the reasoning *behind* the boundaries.

Why might this person be setting boundaries with you? What is the reasoning for not "letting you back in?" What are the real-life events that led to this change? Those are the questions you should be asking if someone creates a boundary with you that you cannot understand. Maybe the truth is that the other person saw something about the relationship with you, or a pattern of behaviors you were engaging in, that wasn't working for them. Maybe they realized that whatever was happening in the relationship was toxic to their life. Perhaps they're not being "mean" by setting boundaries—they're coming from a place of self-love and doing what is best for themselves based on their history with you. Maybe it's not about ego or stubbornness. And if you don't choose to look at these things, you're missing the point. There's no growth, introspection, or self-awareness if you're trying to convince yourself the other person is being "rude." You're refusing to take a good look in the mirror and take any accountability. You're also illustrating exactly why the other person created those boundaries in the first place.

In the boundaries I had to create, I saw the guilt-tripping and name-calling for what it was, which were people upset that I had created boundaries and distanced myself from them. Instead of accepting this new reality, they fought it relentlessly, doing whatever they could to try and get me to feel or act differently. Yet, ironically, they weren't willing to address *why* their actions were unhealthy or do any real reflection on *how* things would be different moving forward. Imagine if I'd broken my boundaries for that! That would be a fake relationship because it would be forced and a way to appease them when I clearly wanted the boundaries I'd instated. Furthermore, I would have been putting myself in harm's way. The boundaries were there to protect me, and I made them for a reason. All this trying in vain to get me to change my mind without them demonstrating any reflection or self-awareness only reinforced the fact that I had done the right thing by establishing the boundaries in the first place.

It's manipulative to call someone "mean" for stating their boundaries because name-calling is an attempt to elicit guilt out of them. You're trying to make them feel badly for setting a boundary and hope they'll feel guilty enough to change their mind. Well, let me tell you something: not only is this manipulative behavior, but it creates a situation in which the other person is *only* going along with you to keep the peace. They don't actually *want* to spend that extra time with you, otherwise they wouldn't have set the boundary to begin with. I know it's probably painful to hear, but if you're trying to force a relationship with anyone, the issue isn't the person or the boundary they set. It's about the unhealthy aspects of the relationship itself (and, perhaps, the unhealthy aspects within yourself that you don't want to look at). And if you don't want to look at that unhealthy part of yourself and your behavior, or do any real reflecting, you don't have to. But then you also have no right to manipulate someone to lower their boundaries. And you shouldn't want to anyway. That would be a fake relationship.

Put it this way: if a friend let you know they needed to take some space from your relationship for their mental health, and they let you know that in a *respectful* way, you'd better hear them loud and clear. It won't serve you or the relationship if you try to dissuade them from their boundaries or try and make them feel badly for needing their space. Because then, if they *did* alter their boundaries for you, you probably wouldn't feel good about spending time with them because you'd know deep down that they wanted space. You'd feel like you were forcing yourself into a situation that you'd been respectfully asked not to be a part of. Then, there's no solid foundation for the relationship. The respect had been eroded because you didn't respect your friend's boundaries and personal needs. The trust had been broken because she wouldn't be able to trust that she could tell you something and you wouldn't try to change it or take advantage of it in some way. And then, enter resentment. She'd begin to resent you because you didn't listen to her and instead put your own needs before hers. And we know that resentment can shatter any real relationship.

Now, in setting boundaries, we need to be clear and direct. We need to properly communicate these boundaries as best we can. We cannot simply assume that others will know where we stand if we don't let them know. That's our job. We can't expect others to respect our boundaries if we haven't properly established them. And once we do, we've done our part. If you've set a boundary and the other person is continually fighting against it, that should tell you something. Take it as information. And it's up to you to decide how you want to engage with any pushback to your boundaries. If you've made them clear, it's not your job to help others cope with their reaction to the boundaries. That's on them.

We need boundaries because we have needs. We need boundaries because they protect us and keep us safe. We need boundaries to ensure that we're putting ourselves first, which is imperative. Anyone who makes you feel badly about having boundaries has an issue with how your boundaries affect *them*. They're not thinking about *you* and what's best for you, they're looking out for themselves. Or perhaps they don't have their own boundaries; if so, that's what they ought to be focusing on.

It's not "dramatic" to set boundaries. It's "dramatic" to call people out for creating boundaries. Boundaries are an act of self-care that can only be created by people who are emotionally mature. The person creating the boundary is *avoiding* drama by protecting themselves from people whose actions aren't good for their mental health. Don't let anyone guilt you out of boundaries that you've created out of your own self-love and care. You made them for a reason.

The truth is, we are fed the lie by our society, and in some cases by our own upbringing, that knowing our worth and acting accordingly somehow makes us selfish or arrogant. Or that it's our job to put others before ourselves. So, then, people mistakenly think that to be a "good person," they must give themselves fully to others, no matter what. They overlook the obvious signs and patterns that should indicate to them that they need boundaries or distance from another person. They neglect their own instincts which tell them they've been hurt, disrespected, or treated unfairly. They cut themselves off from their inner truth because they are desperately trying to "do the right thing." But the right thing according to who? To you? Or to someone else? Because the right thing for *you* would be to not tolerate toxic behavior from others. It would mean not being silent about being mistreated. It would be standing up for yourself and acting accordingly when wronged. Remember that inner child and how she deserves to be treated.

When you're *not* putting up necessary boundaries, you're prioritizing being seen as a good person in the eyes of others or avoiding conflict over doing what is in your best interests. But others may not see your lack of boundaries as you being a "good person." Because others may notice you've been wronged, even if you don't allow yourself to see it. And what that looks like from the outside is that you don't have self-love or value yourself at all. It looks like you have no standards for how to be treated. It looks like you're disconnected from yourself and your truth. It looks like you're playing the game of going along to get along. And not only are you coming across this way to others, but more importantly you're sending *yourself* all these messages. Is that really your goal? Because if your goal is to be a good person, that always starts with being a good person to yourself. And being a good person to yourself means you are conscious, purposeful, and live with intent. It means you protect yourself when you are wronged. It means you put up boundaries wherever and whenever appropriate.

People who don't want to take accountability for their part in things will act astonished when you cut them off. But that reaction does not mean something is wrong with your boundary. And their oblivious reaction should only serve to show you exactly *why* you cut them off. It's their lack of awareness and accountability. It's gaslighting to turn a blind eye to what they may have done that led you to have the reaction that you did. People love to look at the reaction instead of what caused it. News flash: just because someone has a big, loud reaction doesn't mean that *they're* the problem. They may be reacting *to* the problem. So, if you've been cut off from someone's life and have no idea why, perhaps it's time to do some self-reflecting. And maybe, just maybe, ask yourself if you handed them the scissors.

Part of her she kept neatly tucked
In the depths of her soul, too deep
To fit into those pockets of her satin dress
You could miss her by simply staring
Into her eyes, just as they all did
She wasn't someone you could see halfway
Permanently adorned in her aura of authenticity
But if you wanted to truly understand
The depths of her beautiful wholeness
The white and the black
The light and the dark
That she wore so effortlessly
You'd need to be brave enough to allow
The endless layers of her being to unfold
Around you without casting shame
Or disdain, because she has already felt the pain
And carefully put back together all of the pieces
Into an intricate, awe-inspiring masterpiece
She is the author and she holds the pen
And she knows the difference between
Being stared at and being seen.

The Truth Teller

CHAPTER 14

THE TRUTH ABOUT
BEING SEEN

*"Intimacy is being seen and known
as the person you truly are."*
— *Amy Bloom*

L et's begin to zoom into our inner world a bit further. Now that we've discarded our figurative masks and discussed healthy communication, following our own flow and setting healthy boundaries, we're left here with our bare faces. We're probably feeling very vulnerable. This is a good sign because it means we're moving in the right direction. It's time to talk about seeing ourselves and being seen for who we truly are. There's a difference between being stared at and being seen. In today's society, we do a lot of the former and too little of the latter. In our world of reality television, social media, and dating apps, we make it a hobby of staring at others. In fact, not only do we stare at them, but we also make snap judgments about people after a moment's glance in their direction. We don't know who these people actually are, but we *love* to pretend we do. We gossip about what this person's outfit says about their character. We act as if we know everything about every reality show contestant we watch. We make decisions about who to go on dates with by a quick swipe in either direction based on their two-dimensional image. We do a lot of staring but too little seeing.

I'm going to come right out and say it: I've had quite a history of being stared at. And some of it is through my own doing. I put myself on social media. I spent years in the world of the performing arts, prancing around in front of others on stage or auditioning in front of a room full of strangers. I went on countless dates using dating apps before I met my husband. I tend to put myself out there. And I don't mind being stared at, truthfully. As I've mentioned, I'm confident and proud of who I am, inside and out. I'm comfortable facing my own bare-faced reflection, and this comfort extends out to others staring at me as well. But I also know that being stared at doesn't take the place of our deeper need as humans *to be seen.*

I know what it's like to get all the stares but still feel like the loneliest person on the planet. That was me in college. My episodes of Gossip Girl had aired right before I stepped foot on campus my freshman year, and everyone and their mother knew that "Gossip Girl" had arrived on the scene. And yes, my nickname around school became "Gossip Girl." Some of the reactions were genuinely kind (mostly from guys who weren't personally jealous and thought it was fucking cool. And yes, some just wanted to hook up, but I digress). But many of the reactions were anything but kind. Once, I went to the bathroom in my dorm only to find a hand-written note on the back of the stall door that read "Flush the toilet. You know who you are. xoxo, Gossip Girl." My face flushed and I immediately ripped down the sign so that no one else could see it. (By the way, I wasn't the one who didn't flush, but that's irrelevant.) I had a pretty good idea who had written it, because it was obviously the same group of sorority girls who always stared at me and whispered but never said a word to my face. There weren't that many people in the dorm, so it wasn't difficult to figure out. And whenever I walked by them from then on, the looks on their faces confirmed what I knew. I could walk around on campus getting all of the stares in the world, everyone knowing who I was, while simultaneously knowing that very few people actually *knew* me. Because they hadn't ever taken the time to. I was stared at, but I was not genuinely seen.

Staring is easy. It's a quick glance in someone's direction or giving them the good ol' up-and-down. You're taking in an image, but little else. To be seen is to see someone *in full*, behind the curtain of that figurative mask. It's taking the time to see someone for who they are, not just who they present to the world or what your own projections are telling you about them. It's meeting them where they're at, in their natural state. It's trying to understand them and not make assumptions. It's listening, not to respond but to comprehend. It's sitting still with someone and holding space for them as they reveal their deeper layers to you. It's being able to mirror back to someone what you see in them so they know they're being seen.

Why are we talking about feeling seen? Because it's a part of honoring our inner truth and bringing that truth to the surface. There's a wealth of information that lives inside of us that longs to see the light. We innately want to feel that we're seen and loved unconditionally for the people that we are. It's a fundamental need that we all have as human beings. It makes us feel more connected to others in a profound way. We cannot be seen by everyone, nor should we. We don't need to be seen by the stranger who passes us on the street or the person behind us in the grocery checkout aisle. But it is essential that we have at least one other person in our life that can see our true selves and love us for it. Not only do we need that, but we deserve it.

So, in our society where we do a ton of staring, we get accustomed to this way of interacting with others. We mistake being stared at for being seen, so we start to crave more and more of the staring. We don't realize that what we're really looking for goes far beyond being gawked at. We keep trying to fill our cups with the staring in order to satisfy our deeper need to be seen, and it's obviously not working. We continue to put ourselves out there. Maybe if this person gives me attention, I'll feel fulfilled. Maybe if I post this picture, I'll get the likes I need to feel validated. But it never works. It's an endless cycle. Because being stared at isn't what you're craving. To be seen is what we truly need.

When it comes to choosing a romantic partner, or someone to spend your life with, you ought to make sure it's someone who truly sees you. That was something I looked for when, reluctantly, I got on the dating apps in my early twenties. I had moved home temporarily, after college, before I figured out my next steps career-wise. Since I didn't want to meet someone from my hometown and I lived right outside of NYC, I figured the best way for me to meet people would be to use these apps that we all know and hate/love. Well, they can work, let me tell you. Once I got over my ego about not needing an app to meet someone (which was true, I didn't *need* an app to meet someone, but if I hadn't been on the app, I might have never met my husband who was also living just outside of the city at the time), I matched with Matt, my husband.

Now, this is going to sound corny as fuck, but stick with me. I had a gut feeling when I saw his profile for the first time. I was sitting in my childhood bedroom, on my hot pink twin bed from Pottery Barn (yes, let's not talk about it), when I came across his profile. And my inner voice said, "If you swipe right on this guy, it's going to be a good thing." I just knew that I needed to meet him. How did I know? Well, dating isn't as logical as we try and make it out to be. It was beyond the obvious fact that he was a handsome lawyer, with a relatively good fashion sense (I had to spruce him up a bit, but no issues there), a normal-looking group of friends, and a profile without a single red flag. But I sensed he was someone with whom I could feel held. Someone who would—see me.

This was confirmed on our first date a few days later. He was waiting outside for me at the bar in Nyack and when I drove by we locked eyes, and he texted me "Whoa, I think I just saw your beautiful face." And yes, this is the being stared at part, but the moment I walked down that street and into his open arms, I felt like I was somehow returning home. He held me for a few moments that felt like hours and seconds all at once. And then comes the being seen. We sat across from one another over gin and tonics at the back booth of the bar. His eyes never left me once, and he was taking in every single syllable I uttered. I felt my natural energy pouring out, without a need or desire to hold back in any way. There was only the urge to share more because I felt completely safe and understood. We spoke about every topic under the moon and stars that night. In our four-hour conversation, we touched on family, spirituality, career paths, religion, friendships, love, and everything in between. The words flowed like streamers. And I felt completely *seen and held*.

Needless to say, we each deleted our dating apps right afterward and our relationship began. We both knew, intrinsically. He was my male counterpart. He felt like home. He saw me for exactly who I was and he loved me for all of it. With him, I never wanted to hide. With him, I could be my full self and live in my full expression. Matt makes me feel proud to be who I am, and he's never asked me to change any aspects of my true self for him. He loves me in full. He is in awe of me, and he consistently tells me that. He knows me intrinsically, inside and out, because he has made it his mission to do so. He makes me excited to be all that I am. And there is no love more deeply fulfilling than that.

In any healthy relationship, you want to feel seen. Because being seen means that you're being your authentic self. And if you want a lasting relationship with someone who loves you for the person that you are, you'll want to prioritize this concept of feeling "seen." You know you're seen when you're the same self with the other person that you are when you're by yourself. There are no mincing of words or calculations involved. There is no mask. You're free to be yourself and you aren't feeling shamed out of that in any way. Because, truthfully, if you're not being yourself in a relationship, then you're not in a genuine relationship at all. How do you know the person likes you for you when you aren't even *being* you? Exactly, you don't. The only way to know whether you're loved unconditionally is if you're being your authentic self.

I take this concept of being "seen" with me into my other relationships as well. Not every friendship or family relationship will be equally as deep and profound, but there is something to be said about being able to be your true self within a relationship. And, oftentimes, the reason that relationships fall off is due to a lack of authenticity and transparency on either or both sides. When you withhold your truth from yourself, it creates distance in your relationships. When you're wearing a mask, you create separation between yourself and the other person. The more honest you are with yourself, the more honest you are with others. So, if you're wondering why your relationships don't feel fulfilling, or why you don't feel "seen," ask yourself if you're really seeing yourself first.

It's also not your job to prove your self-worth to those who cannot or have refused to see you for who you are. There will be people who are committed to misunderstanding you. They want to think a certain way about you and hold on tightly to that inaccurate perception because it makes them feel safe. They'd rather not have their image of you challenged because that would require them to look at *their* deeper issues, which are not about you, but about whatever shit they're projecting onto you. The story they're telling themselves derives from how their insecurities come alive when they're around you. And they can't tolerate those feelings, so they project onto you or others whatever story helps them sleep at night. You deserve people in your life who take the time and make the effort to see you for your true essence. Not the "you" they think they know based on other people's gossip. Or the "you" they project from their own insecurities or unresolved trauma. Or the "you" they gather from staring in your direction. Or the "you" they knew from ten years ago who's evolved a great deal since then. You deserve those who want more of you and who don't have any misperceptions about who you are. You deserve to be seen, in full.

Because we can all be stared at. We stare in the direction of others every time we leave the house—unless we're just lost in our own worlds—in which case, WAKE UP! But don't confuse staring and seeing. One has only to do with our packaging, and the other with who we are deep down.

To see someone is the greatest gift you can give to them.

When you're not making the time and effort to see others, you're losing out on valuable information. And it's dangerous to operate on such little information. You may think you know the people you're associating with better than you actually do. You may be projecting what you want to see on a person and keep people around, or conversely cut them off, based on these inaccurate projections. The more you see someone, the less you'll be confused or feel uncomfortable with them. Perhaps you need to sit with the discomfort of meeting the gaze of the other and holding that gaze. Because the quicker you turn away, the less information you'll really have about the other person. But again, it begins with being able to stare at your own reflection without immediately looking away.

Being seen requires time and effort, both of which seem to be in short supply in today's world. *Make* the time. Put in the effort. It's a choice. And if you're not choosing it, well, what a shame that is indeed. Staring will keep you on the surface with no real connection to those around you. Being seen allows us a deeper connection to ourselves, others, and the world at large. It's what we long for and need. We've discarded those figurative masks for a reason. Here's to seeing and to being seen.

Sometimes when I feel like a block of sandpaper
Is rasping away at my throat
And the sides of my jaw are aching like they've
Been gnawing away at a huge wad
Of sticky, dense gum for years
I parade my mind over there

To that spot in the middle of the beige, suede couch where
I melt into a canopy of cushions
Bubbie's the only other person in the room
She's reading, a Newsweek flopped across
Her velvety periwinkle peddle-pushers
A glass of Pino Grigio cupped between her
Diamond-clad fingers
It's four o'clock, of course

And I'm breathing in her powdery, dandelion scent
That's seeped into all her home furnishings
As I listen to the dim moan of the laundry machines
By the side door, which is the front door
Of my Bubbie's house. My laundry's in there
I've brought it home in a cluster of plastic bags
As I always do when I come to visit Bubbie
On a weekend from school

Bubbie's got a standing offer to do my laundry, any laundry
And every piece of laundry I might want done so that
I can feel collected when I reenter my school dorm
After having spent the weekend at her house
It could be any weekend and if I had it my way it would be
Every.

I've got my feet cradled in the fur of her rug
In the family room, where we're sitting, where there's
No place in the room you can look without seeing
A bundle of pictures, each one in its own bold colored
Or beaded frame, and I'm basking in the sun
That's gleaming through the glass doors to the open yard
As I'm pressed delicately into my canopy of cushions

Sun still swept over my tiny body and I'm
Trying not to close my eyes, as I trace them over
And over again across the room to let it seep into me
In its entirety, so that I have this moment
When it's hard to swallow
The pounding in the back of my throat
When it's impossible to quiet
The throbbing in my skull
I can close my eyes and drown into
My canopy.

The Truth Teller, written in 2011 at Trinity College

CHAPTER 15

THE TRUTH ABOUT
VALUES

"The more awake one is to the material world, the more one is asleep to spirit."

—Rumi

L et's circle back to the grounding chapter. I've always held my values close because they're part of my foundation. Case example: the poem before the chapter is about my Bubbie's old house in Longmeadow, Massachusetts. I valued my visit's to Bubbie's house so much that I'd frequently visit her on my winter and spring breaks in High School. I'd have regularly scheduled lunch dates with Bubbie during college, and one of the reasons I picked the school I did was because it was a 25-minute drive from my Bubbie. Why? Because my relationship with Bubbie was one I always valued. I cherished every moment I got.

The truth about values is that many people don't have them. They *think* they do. They fool themselves into thinking that, by following whatever is trendy or popular in the moment, they're in line with some sort of value system. That's all an enormous crock of BS. Because truthfully, if you have a solid sense of values, they don't change from season to season. They're not influenced by what an influencer tells you to care about. They come from within and they're an integral part of your foundation. You can see them reflected in the choices you make and the individuals you keep around you. That is, if you have them.

We found out a lot about people's values during the pandemic. This is why many relationships dissolved, became distanced, or conversely evolved into something greater over this period in time. When a tragedy hits, you're going to undoubtedly find out a heck of a lot about a person's sense of what's important based on the decisions that they make. We saw all sorts of reactions from our family and friends during the pandemic. And listen, there's no "right way" to go through a collective trauma. None of us were prepared. But that's not the point. The point is that our personal choices, and the way that we react to what life throws our way, reveals truth about ourselves and what we value. And it's essential to have a solid value system to guide you through life. It forms the basis of your roadmap, with each path you choose directing you towards something you value dearly. If we don't have these values, what are we basing our decisions on?

When we don't have a solid set of values to guide us, we often wind up at a destination that doesn't speak to us. We end up surrounded by objects and people and situations that aren't aligned with who we are. And we wonder how we got there. But if, along the way, we're following the flow of others instead of our own, we're being led by *their* values. It's a sobering moment when you realize that your values don't align with those of certain individuals you keep close. Because then you're left with the question: what is your relationship based on? Sometimes, you'll find it's based on circumstances that have kept you in close physical proximity, or it's simply your shared history that's held your relationship together. And nothing else.

So, does this mean we need to discard any relationship that doesn't align with our values? Not necessarily. But it does mean you need to be careful with those boundaries. This way, you can maintain what's important to you whilst you're in the relationship. But if you're needing to *compromise* your values for a relationship, well, I think you already know the answer to that one. No healthy relationship would ask you to sacrifice what you personally value. Of course, healthy relationships also may assist in your growth, and you may find you're beginning to value different things over time. That's okay. Just make sure they're in line with how you feel within so that your internal self isn't conflicted with your external circumstances.

You can find out a lot about a person and what they value by the people, places, and things they have in their life. Are the individuals around them people who share the same values? Are those people respectful, honest, genuine, and loyal? Do they go deep? Are the places they frequent meaningful to them or are they just "doing it for the gram"? Are they surrounded by meaningless objects and clutter as a stand-in for real purpose and fulfillment? Well, maybe it's because they don't have a value-system, or they do but their values consist of things like getting the applause from strangers on Instagram or doing whatever is most popular that week. Ain't that a sad truth.

It's always served me well whenever I make decisions grounded in my values. I'm very close with my family and I value my time with them, so I live five minutes away from my parents and ten minutes from my brother and his soon-to-be wife. I value helping people, so I'm a therapist for a living. I value the inner work, so I make time to reflect on my feelings regularly. I value personal growth, so I'm always reading, writing, and traveling. I value creativity, so I express that through fashion, social media, interior design (yes, my apartment) and more. I value health and wellness, so I exercise and maintain a healthy lifestyle. I value relationships in which I can be myself without having to restrict myself in some way, so I distance myself or set appropriate boundaries around relationships where I'm being asked to tone myself down. Basically, I make time for what I value. That's how I make my life feel like my own.

You can't be aligned in your own truth if you aren't grounded in what you value. In fact, you'll be out of alignment if you don't know what it is you stand for. You'll find that making decisions becomes difficult because you don't have a fundamental set of beliefs to guide you. You'll be easily swept away in the cacophony of conflicting opinions in the world if you don't know where you stand. As one of my favorite song lyrics, written by The Script, says, *"If you don't stand for something, you'll fall for anything."* Be about something. Have an opinion. If not, you're in danger of being swayed and misled by those who have ulterior motives.

So, how do we discover what our own values are? Well, like anything else, you need to look within for the answers. No one else can tell you what you value. They can tell you what you *should* value (and don't we all know people who love to do so). But it's not a personal value unless it's something you can consistently stand by and believe in, regardless of where you're at and the company you keep. Your values, as part of your grounding, are there for you to return to when you are feeling empty, lost, or in search of meaning. As I've said, some of my core values are self-love and respect, personal growth, authenticity, family, close friends, quality over quantity, health, honesty, creativity, and truth. I allow these values to guide me in my decision-making, and I return to them whenever I want to be reminded of my purpose and meaning. They help me understand who is meant to be in my life and who isn't because I have a personal template for what I believe in and what I will and won't tolerate in my life. I feel a sense of pride when I make choices that are in line with my values because I know that ad-hering to those values is what's best for me.

There's nothing like being proud of who you are and what you stand for.

And I mean that. Nothing. Most insecure people I know, if not all of them, don't stand for anything. They don't know what they value and thus they flitter around from one idea to the next. It's hard to take someone like that seriously because you can tell they don't take *themselves* seriously. When you don't have a solid foundation of values, you're giving off the impres-sion that you lack confidence and a sense of self. You become someone who follows the crowd because you're lost, rather than an individual of substance who has something unique to offer the world. It's the people who lack a solid sense of who they are and what they're all about who fill up their lives with distractions. Oh, maybe this new designer bag will fill me up with meaning. Maybe if I get this procedure then I'll feel whole. Perhaps if I do whatever I can to remain in this friend group then I won't feel lonely. Maybe if I marry this person I will have a sense of purpose or identity. But all of these substi-tutes for being grounded as an individual are temporary and unfulfilling. No material item is going to fill the void within. No vacation is going to make up for the fact that you'll return home to the same place of emptiness. No relationship is going to fulfill you if you can't first find that fulfillment within your-self.

There is no true happiness or fulfillment in a life void of values. If you're not grounded in your values, it'll surely catch up with you. You will always be confused about who you truly are. You won't be proud of your actions when you reflect on them. Ask yourself: Are you proud of who you are? If you can't honestly answer that question with a resounding "YES!"—then it doesn't matter how proud you are of the "stuff" you have. The material objects around you are never going to fulfill you. They won't fill up your empty soul. If you aren't proud of who you are and aren't living in alignment with your values, the rest doesn't even matter. It's meaningless. You'll always crave the next handbag or destination. You'll always be searching. Because you're looking for fulfillment in all the wrong places. You have nothing grounding you. Without values, you have no road map. You are lacking an inner compass. And we sure as hell all need a compass to guide us, don't we?

So consider what it is you value. What drives your decision making? What truths do you hold internally that you can be sure of? What do you find innately important? These are the building blocks of your values. Reflect on them often and come back to them. Call them to mind when you're making decisions. That is how you act in alignment with the person you are and what you believe in. That is how you can stand for something instead of being swayed by the values, or lack thereof, of others. Be about something. Stop fooling yourself into thinking that the things you own have any intrinsic value. They're simply stand-ins for what really matters.

All these beings running on fumes
Sprinting toward an unreachable abyss
No sense of direction
No solid ground beneath their blistered feet
No face mask to cover their deceit
They're utterly exhausted and they don't know why
While they trade in sleep for Pilates machines
Thinking that this is the way to achieve their dreams
And they post their polished, plastered smiles
Then they put their phones down and cry for a while
Deeply depleted, in desperate need
Of nourishment from the inside out
While they're focused on the outside in
What kind of world are we living in?

The Truth Teller

CHAPTER 16

THE TRUTH ABOUT

RUNNING
ON EMPTY

"We are a culture of people who've bought into the idea that if we stay busy enough, the truth of our lives won't catch up with us."
—Brené Brown (@brenebrown)

L et's take a closer look at the speed at which we move along that roadmap of ours. What's your general pace of life? Funny, you may not have stopped to observe this before. But it's vital information. Your pace of life is speaking to you, and you need to listen to it. How people start off their day says a lot about the way they go through the rest of it. When someone, for example, begins their day with a morning run, they usually don't stop running once they're done on said run. (Unless, of course, they make a conscious effort to center themselves and change pace for the rest of the day.) They run throughout their day. They run from one thing to the next, limbs flailing and minds clogged with their endless to-do lists. Their general pace of life is running. They know exactly what they will be doing each minute of the week and if they don't, they panic. They don't want any possibility of a blank space in their day because that space in time will mean stillness. And they cannot face the threat of stillness because they are remarkably afraid of being still. They don't want to sit still because then they will have to face themselves. They will have to embody themselves.

These days, many of us are scared to embody our full selves. We're scared of what we might find and how we'll feel if we do so. Because being able to run away and escape the tender, awkward, shameful feelings we hold deep within—stuffed down and out of awareness—is the only way we've ever known. But we need, we desperately *need*, to find a new way. Because it's literally killing us. We're walking around without an ounce of understanding of what is below the surface, and we wonder why we feel so out of touch. We need to tune in. Collectively, we're disconnected from ourselves and each other. We're racing around without a thought as to what is going on within. We don't know how we feel. We don't know why things *aren't working*. We don't know *why* we're doing the things we do. And we're often too afraid to know.

The truth is that our attention span as a society is decreasing to the speed of a thirty-second TikTok video. We've become a culture of instant gratification and of distracting ourselves from our pain. It's easier, isn't it? Instead of sitting with our feelings, we can just scroll through Instagram to avoid what's going on with us internally. And when we have all of these pacifiers for our feelings, like prank videos on social media, then we continue to reinforce this need to move away from any negative emotion we're experiencing. This is why so many of us distracted and numbed our way through the pandemic. It was all we could do to pass the time.

And this is because our society runs on empty. Instead of fueling ourselves with proper self-care, which includes feeling our feelings and making space for them, people are running away from themselves as fast as they can. They don't even know what it is they're running toward. They just don't want to be where they currently are, so they'll do anything to escape their own reflection. It doesn't help that our culture glamorizes productivity and the grind.

We've somehow forgotten the fact that attending to our emotional experience and working on self-development is the most productive work of all.

Not only is the busyness of life expected, but it's encouraged. We applaud those who accomplish the seemingly unfathomable. We pride ourselves on having an overflowing social calendar. The more, the better. Go big or go home. I'll sleep when I'm dead. Well, hate to tell you, but ya' *look* dead! You might be waking up every day at 5:00 a.m. to run eight miles and tackle the first ten things on your to-do list by 7 a.m., but your eye bags are sagging down your cheeks. If that's what you're dealing with, it's time to ask yourself if your routine is serving you. If you're looking at yourself in the mirror and can't *see* yourself because all you see is the exhaustion from hanging on by a thread, well, this is a sign that you might have lost yourself.

There is a difference between a healthy hustle and spreading yourself thin. Having drive and working hard are things to be proud of. But working yourself to the bone, at the expense of other important areas in your life, is not healthy or productive. If you're pouring yourself fully into your career bucket and pouring little to nothing into your relationship or mental health bucket—well, you're not going to be able to continue the hustle for long. It'll catch up with you. Your health will decline whether you like it or not. Your relationships will begin to crumble as you continue to neglect the time and effort they require. The sprint is just that—a sprint. There's an endpoint, and it's not too far down the road.

We need to consider the motivation for all this running. Because when you're sprinting through life, it prompts the question: Why the speed? You're not always on the clock, so if it's self-imposed, there's a reason. What are you running from? What are you running toward? Well, chronic running can stem from a place of emptiness inside. It often stems from an insatiable need to fill the void within. It's the intense fear of sitting still with yourself. It's not being able to see that you have intrinsic value as a human being that has nothing to do with the things you achieve. It's the running away from trauma and toward an unknown abyss that we frantically tell ourselves will somehow be better than where we are now. We're running away from ourselves and even further away with every check off on our never-ending to-do list. Whatever you can busy yourself with, there you are. You're everywhere and yet nowhere. And then, you're never truly happy because, truth is, you can't be happy if you're not ever living in the present moment. We've gone over this: happiness exists in the present.

People are running towards happiness and success as if they are destinations. They wonder why they're still unhappy, even after they've accomplished all their daily tasks and then some. But what if the formula for happiness and success was not embedded in these to-do lists? After all, we are the ones who create them. Perhaps there are tasks on our lists that aren't necessary. Maybe we've said "yes" to engagements that we don't, deep down, really want to attend. Perhaps we've over-stuffed our calendars with things that don't speak to us or bring us joy. Maybe more isn't always better. Maybe the key is selectivity. Perhaps we should be more intentional when we create our to-do lists in the first place and ask ourselves if each item on the list is actually worth doing. Furthermore, if your head is always down as you run from task to task, then you're probably not able to be fully present for each one. You can't rush through your days and expect to be fully awake to each moment before you. This is where you can apply the mentality of quality over quantity. Perhaps the key is to have fewer items on your to-do list, and to make it your objective to be as present as you can be each step of the way. Because, if you get to the end of your day and you can't remember the details of anything, then what was the point?

The lie we tell ourselves is that we can continue running forever. We think we can evade our feelings or any unpleasant situation if we run fast enough. If we just book enough vacations or drink enough cocktails or schedule that extra workout, *then* we'll be happy. Well, then why do you feel empty and depleted? Why is it that when someone asks you how you're feeling, you don't know how to respond? I'll tell you why: because you don't know the answer. You can't know the answer to how you're feeling if you haven't spent any time *with* your feelings. So, unless you want to be a robot, you're going to have to find a way to slow the fuck down.

That is, if you want to feel better. Because distracting yourself and healing yourself are not the same thing—at all. It takes introspection and self-awareness to heal. Trying not to think unpleasant thoughts or feelings is just pushing them temporarily out of your awareness and into your body and subconscious where they'll get stored. They'll fester and come out in an ugly way when you least expect it. You might think you're escaping something unfavorable by dodging these feelings, but there's no way to escape what hasn't been directly faced and processed. You have to work through them, and that means facing your fears head on. It means asking yourself the honest questions: What am I running from? What am I running toward?

And until you face whatever that is, you'll be running from the truth and, eventually, you'll trip over your shoelace and be forced to face the inevitable crash. We simply cannot run away from ourselves. We can't outrun our truth. It's always there, whispering in our ear and grumbling in our gut, trying in vain to make itself heard. So until you consciously decide to give yourself permission to slow down and process, just know that you're not really accomplishing anything of substance. Busyness doesn't equal productivity. Busyness doesn't equal happiness. Busyness doesn't equal success. It is just keeping yourself in perpetual motion while you neglect the real and productive work within.

Pops of pink and purple
Peeping through the greenery
Vines curling amongst the petals
Pitter-pattering with the breeze
It was something of a canopy
Sprawled around her hammock
Cradling her in its delicacy
Grounding her in its entirety
It is a living masterpiece
Growing alongside her
In unison as the edges blur
As she sits enveloped in the natural
Mother Earth is truly radical

The Truth Teller

CHAPTER 17

THE TRUTH ABOUT
GROWTH

"The degree to which a person can grow is directly proportional to the amount of truth they can accept about themselves without running away."
– Leland Val Van De Wall

The funny thing about growth is that, as exciting as it may seem on the surface, so many of us are desperately afraid of it. I used to be. As I mentioned earlier, throughout my youth, I was terrified of growing up. The entire concept of adulting scared the living shit out of me. I didn't have any older siblings to pave the way for me. I was lucky enough to have a beautiful childhood that I did not want to part from. The future was unknown and the unknown always scared me. I wanted things to stay the same. Part of my eating disorder was an attempt to keep my body the same, because if that was the only thing I could control, then I was going to do whatever I could to do so. I'd try and stop time if I could. Well, we already know how that turned out.

I thought I'd always be afraid of growth. The word itself made me itch from the inside out. While I thought that I could consciously avoid growth by keeping myself safe and small, I realized even then that time was passing regardless of my attempts to thwart it. I could either evolve with the passing of time, or I could remain the same and eventually fall behind. And falling behind was something I was not willing to do. In fact, part of the reason I was able to recover from my eating disorder was my fear of falling behind. It was the summer before college when I began my true recovery once I made the conscious decision that I was not going to allow my disorder to hold me back from my peers. I'd go to college like the rest of them, no matter what it took.

The interesting thing I came to realize about growth is that what's scarier than growing is not to grow at all. The idea that I'd need to defer my college acceptance just to sit in my childhood bedroom for a semester or a year while I battled anorexia was a nightmare concept. The shame that boiled in my veins at the thought of it was enough to abandon the thought entirely. I wasn't going to allow that to be an option. Suddenly, the idea of facing my fears head-on became way more appealing than giving into the fear itself. There's no potential in staying the same. And I knew I had potential. And I sure as hell wasn't going to sleep on it.

What I've learned over time about growth is that it's a conscious and personal choice. Not all of us are growing. And as I've evolved, I've been able to easily weed out relationships that aren't growing alongside me. I can spot those who are remaining the same. And, usually, those who are afraid of change aren't going to be those cheering you on in your growth. They're intimidated by it. And if you're not careful, and you don't set proper boundaries around these people (or remove yourself completely from the relationship if it's toxic or impacts your growth negatively), then you could be allowing their fear to thwart your progress.

The truth is that not everyone wants to grow. Many people, if not most, are content living as they are. They're addicted to the drug of comfort. They're not interested in putting in that extra work on themselves to figure out why they hold themselves back and people-please their way through life. Or they're paralyzed by fear and limiting beliefs. They've made an existence out of running away from their truth and, ultimately, from themselves. The unknown of it all can be enough to make them want to remain as they are. So, not everyone wants to grow. And it's important for us to know this, because knowing it will save us a lot of frustration and heartache.

Sometimes we find ourselves growing in a different direction from someone we once felt very connected with. It can be confusing and bring up a lot of mixed emotions. That's natural. But then we get scared. We're afraid of the changes that come with this newfound growth. We don't want to face the inevitable loss and separation that comes along with growth. Especially the loss and separation from that former version of ourselves. So, we hang on for dear life. We try to stay stagnant. We try and minimize the ways in which we've changed. We file down our edges. We try and stay in our old box, where things felt safe. But the consequence of filing down your growth is that you're self-sabotaging. There's a personal sacrifice you're making when you thwart your progress. When a relationship, with yourself or others, cannot withstand the natural ebbs and flows of life, all you can do is acknowledge it and allow it to occur. The alternative is losing ourselves. And after all of that inner work you've been doing, are you really going to let that be an option?

When we're committed to our growth, we inevitably want to share that growth with our loved ones. We want to take them with us and share with them our newfound knowledge and have the pleasure of their company along the ride. Why wouldn't we? But then we discover that not everyone is interested in coming along that growth journey with us. And sometimes that leads to outgrowing those who aren't interested in growing. (They don't call it growing pains for no reason).

Growing goes hand in hand with outgrowing.

When we outgrow people and things along the way, it doesn't mean we are doing anything wrong. We are simply undergoing the natural process of growth itself.

It's a conscious choice to grow. It's something you have to give yourself permission to do. You also have to give yourself permission to outgrow those who aren't growing. Letting go can be painful, but it's far more painful to stay in a relationship where you're not being seen or met. Growth is an individual endeavor. You can't grow for someone else. Growth starts with becoming aware, laying the foundation of who you are and what you want your life to be about, and then giving yourself *permission* to go after it. The part about growth that we often don't talk about is loss. Growth comes with loss. When you're growing and those around you are not or are growing in a different direction, there's going to be a fall-off. And since we don't anticipate that fall-off, we think we are doing something wrong. Others might tell us so. "Why isn't she still friends with that person?" I'll tell you why that might be.

Because when you're leveling up, you're not the same person you once were. So why would you have all of the same relationships as you progress? When you grow, your needs change. And this includes your needs within relationships. Maybe you've become less dependent on the approval of others. Maybe you've learned to value yourself enough not to give your energy away so freely to people who don't reciprocate. Maybe you're no longer willing to water down and sugarcoat shit to stay on "good terms" with others. And what is wrong with that? Nothing at all. The only people who have a problem with it are those who benefited from the way you used to be, or who are intimidated by your growth.

The thing about growth is that it's full of unknowns. And that's what's terrifying and electrifying about it. Think about those old monkey bars on our childhood playground. You're in between bars and one hand is clutching the bar you hang from while the other is temporarily suspended in the air. In a similar way, you're reaching for the rung ahead on your growth path, but for a second there you don't know what it is you're reaching for. You're swimming in space for a moment, trusting that somehow you will find your way and make it to the next bar. Growth requires trust. You must trust in yourself and in whatever higher power you believe in (or whatever it is you believe in) that you will make it through. You have to trust that you will successfully reach the next bar so you can release the previous one and wind up where you're meant to be.

I actually came up with this concept of the monkey bars back when I was recovering from my eating disorder. I felt suspended in space with my hand outstretched toward the next chapter. I obviously didn't know what college would look like, as I'd never been. Even more so, I didn't know what college would look like while recovering from an eating disorder. I had to trust and believe in myself that I could rise to the occasion. I remember the first day of school, moving day, after my parents had helped me hang up all my posters and make the bed. All there was left to do was say our "see you laters." They'd already let me know the conditions: that I could stay at school as long as I was able to keep my weight stable and show that I was moving forward in my recovery. That was a tall order for an eighteen-year-old leaving home for the first time! But they trusted me enough to give me the shot. And, even more importantly, I trusted *myself*. And as I sat there on the bed with my mom as my dad went to get the car, we embraced in the heavy, anticipatory silence. Neither of us knew what the next few days or weeks would look like. All we had was our shared trust and belief in who I am and who I always have been. That I'm someone who rises to the occasion whenever I set my mind to it. And just like that, I ripped off the Band-Aid and pulled out of the hug and let her know: "It's okay. You can go now. I'll call you later." And just like that, I began my four-year college journey and continued my recovery successfully. All because I trusted myself and I gave myself permission to move forward.

You're not going to know exactly what your growth journey will look like, especially before you set out on it. You can try and map it out and picture it in your mind's eye, but the truth is that you must have an innate trust in yourself and be willing to embrace the unknown. And yes, growth means letting go of comfort. Comfort will come to you, but it isn't something to grasp on to. True comfort arises internally when you realize you can trust yourself. What's comforting is showing yourself that you can do what you put your mind to. That's the most comforting thought of all.

Choose growth. Because if you don't, life will continue to grow around you. Just because you decide not to grow doesn't mean those around you won't. Just because you decide not to grow doesn't mean the clock isn't ticking as one day rolls into the next. And, eventually, you likely won't feel that sense of safety in remaining the same. Because your life won't be the same when those around you choose to grow in their own directions. And ultimately, you will never regret growth. But you will regret remaining the same while the world grows around you. Keep your eyes on the monkey bars ahead of you and, while you're at it, trust the process.

Another gone that once was near
And she's frozen in her bath of fear
The panic that swells from deep within
It steals the breath right out of her skin

And just like that, like grains of fallen sand
Summer slipping like a faded tan
Between her fingertips, upon which sits
The friendship bracelet that still fits

They wonder what she did this time
To make that list of friends decline
Must be some internal flaw she has
Otherwise, wouldn't her friendships last?

And as she's moaning in her pain
They meet her eyes with disdain
As she unties the bracelet from her wrist
What part of the story did they miss?

The Truth Teller

CHAPTER 18

THE TRUTH ABOUT
LOSING FRIENDS

"Your expansion and growth may be uncomfortable for many, but not everyone is coming with you. Keep going."
—Yasmine Cheyenne (@yasminecheyenne)

So, now that we've talked about growing, let's expand upon something we commonly outgrow: friendships. Friendship fallouts are experiences most of us have that we don't like to talk about. But we should, because it's so common that doing so could really help us connect in a deeper way. Losing friends is a natural part of life. It means that we are growing. It means that, personally and collectively, we are evolving as we form more mature relationships that reflect who we are as individuals in our most elevated form. That reflect the people we were naturally born to be.

Naturally, we as people move in different directions. And while some friends come along on our journeys, some won't. So, when we start to notice that we are growing apart from old friends, sometimes there's a tendency to want to overlook the issues within the friendship. Why? Because you want the friendship to remain the same. It's hard to acknowledge when a relationship devolves into something that feels less meaningful to you. But the worst thing you can do for yourself when you notice that something has changed in a friendship is to overlook it. If this is a serious issue that conflicts with your values, then you ought to take a serious look at it. If you hold onto relationships that have run their course, you're setting yourself up for disappointment. If you can only keep the relationship together by overlooking serious issues, then you can be sure those issues will be the end of the relationship.

Freshman year of college, I was friends with a group of girls. They were fun, energetic, and always had something going on. Friends with all the fraternity brothers, we bopped from one frat to the next and hosted huge pre-games in our dorm rooms beforehand. I was never without plans with this friend group. There wasn't a party we weren't at. But somewhere along the line, I learned there were some group dynamics that weren't healthy and I didn't want to be involved in it any longer. I had a decision to make. Continue to hang out with these girls because they were fun to party with, even if that meant going against my better judgment and being treated in a way I didn't think was fair, or take my own route. You already know what I did. My own route it was, baby!

It wasn't easy to distance myself from this group. I hadn't had any time to make other friends. I knew that walking away meant being in limbo land for a while in the social sense. But I was able to hang onto that monkey bar in front of me because I intuitively knew it was in my best interests to move on. And sometimes moving on is what we need to do. How do we know when a relationship has run its course? When we don't feel we are being heard. When our personal, emotional, or physical self is in danger in any way. When we are being mistreated. These are all very valid reasons for relationships of any sort to end.

If someone is willing to let a relationship with you go because they're too afraid or couldn't be bothered to put in the effort, that's not someone worth having in your life. Quite frankly, the relationship clearly lacked substance and depth if when you bring up real feelings you're met with silence, dismissiveness, or anything of the sort. Healthy relationships involve open communication and mutual effort. If a relationship can't withstand those conversations, it speaks to the lack of strength and longevity of the relationship. What it should tell you is that you can't rely on this person to meet you where you're at. The relationship, then, will not feel balanced. You probably won't feel heard.

Many of us believe that the number of friends we have is somehow a statement on who we are as individuals. And it is, in a way. But not in the way you might think. Having a lot of friends doesn't mean you're "better" or "cooler" or "happier" or "more successful" than those who don't have as many friends. In fact, you can be an incredibly successful person and only have one or two close friends. Conversely, you can be someone who isn't growing at all and have more friends than you can count. Friendships don't define you, and they shouldn't. You define you. I know it can be scary to walk away from a relationship that's no longer serving you. But remember that your best friend is that inner child of yours. And if your inner child is upset and isn't feeling respected or heard, remember that it's going to come out in an unhealthy way. You're not a failure if a relationship doesn't work out.

You aren't defined by any relationship aside from the one you have with yourself.

Never compromise your sense of self-worth for a relationship. Remember to have standards in your friendships. Go back to your value system. Do you value openness and honesty? If so, that should hold true in your friendships. You should be able and willing to discuss issues as they arise, which they inevitably will because that's how relationships work. Do you value trust? Then you should be able to trust that your friends will have your back even when you're not around. You should be able to trust that if your friends have an issue with you, that they'll work it out with you instead of ghosting you. Do you value respect? Then your friends should respect you. Point blank.

Let's talk about what we gain when we walk away from a relationship that's no longer serving us. We gain self-respect. We respect the decision that we made to walk away, and we can be genuinely proud of that decision. We gain an opportunity to move forward and be open to other relationships that serve us better. We can take time to process what did or didn't work out in the relationship so that we gain a deeper understanding of ourselves. In walking away from relationships that are no longer serving us, we are taking our inner children by the hand and walking them toward safety. You will never regret walking away from a relationship that's run its course.

What I've learned about friendships is that having healthy ones is really important. And it's come to be something I value greatly. As much as I believe in the importance of having a strong sense of who you are as an individual, we also exist in this world with other people and it's meaningful to have relationships with those people. My best friend, who knows who she is, is someone who has proven time and again that she genuinely and deeply cares about me. She listens to what I have to say and remembers it all. She follows up. She calls. She checks in. She's always happy for my happiness. She takes it very seriously when I bring up something that's bothering me, and she wants to make it better. And having a friend like this has really shown me how important it is to value the friends who show up. The ones who put in the effort. The genuine ones are gems.

LOSING FRIENDS

So, how do you know if you have true friends? Well, you wouldn't have to question it if you did. It's the people you can be fully yourself with. The people who you can trust with everything inside of you. The people who keep it honest with you and who encourage you to be your best self. The people who will listen to you cry or vent. The people who don't talk shit behind your back. The people who make the effort to check in on you and spend quality time with you and not just when it's convenient for them. The people who are genuinely happy for your happiness and accomplishments. Of course, there are all sorts of friendships, and they don't have to be equally deep. But if you can't be yourself in a friendship and be respected for who you are, then maybe it isn't the friendship for you. And maybe, just maybe, that's okay.

My throat bleeds with the remains
Of explanations and exclaims
Can they hear me?
Is it an effort in vain?
I contort myself in utter pain
Rinsing out the suds of shame
Desperate for things to be the same

A terrifying weight compresses my chest
All of my efforts seem to be in jest
Perhaps it's time to begin to digest
To accept what is and let go of the protest
Of the unheard words that I'd expressed
And release my truth that's been suppressed
And suddenly I am free of all distress.

The Truth Teller

CHAPTER 19

THE TRUTH ABOUT
ACCEPTANCE

"Accept people as they present themselves to you, not who your mind wants them to be."
— Omar Hachem (@iamomarhachem)

We often think acceptance means agreement. We think that if we are to accept something someone says to us, or a situation that didn't work out how we wanted it to, it means that we're "giving up" or, worse, that we're a "failure." Society instills the message that we should keep pushing through, at all costs.

Acceptance is often seen as giving up or giving in. But acceptance doesn't mean that you're saying everything is "okay" or that you can't handle the situation at hand. It just means you're surrendering from trying to control or change things that are clearly going to stay the way they are—which is an effort in vain.

Also, no one needs to know you've accepted anything or anyone. The acceptance part is for you, so you can move along in peace.

Acceptance is a natural part of life. At some point or another, you're going to have to accept something you can't change or control. Maybe it's a relationship that isn't working out the way that you'd once hoped. Maybe it's a certain career path that isn't going well. Or maybe it's the loss of someone that you love. That last one is something I recently faced. I had to accept the passing of my Bubbie this past year. It was something I'd dreaded for as long as I can remember. I always knew that because my relationship with Bubbie was so deep and that she was one of the closest people to me, that it was going to be extraordinarily painful for me to say goodbye to her one day. I also knew that, as part of life, it was inevitable.

So, I started preparing myself for it. Emotionally, that is. Every time I'd see her, especially as she was getting older, I'd treat it as if it were the last time. I'd tell her how much I loved her. I'd take pictures with her. I always made sure she was fully updated on everything in my life. I made sure that I was fully present with her. My mom intuitively knew that since this was going to be so difficult for me (and her, of course), that she needed to be transparent with me when Bubbie started to decline. Of course, in the moment, I'd get upset with her from time to time. It wasn't easy hearing all the harsh details. But she knew that sugar-coating or leaving out important information was only going to set me up for complete shock when the inevitable occurred.

I was not in shock. I was prepared. By the time the moment came, and I got the call, I'd already spent hours upon hours crying, journaling, and talking to loved ones about my feelings. I'd written my eulogy for Bubbie's funeral, which was something that was incredibly important to me. I wanted to honor my Bubbie in the best way that I could, through my words (which she had always adored). Speaking at the funeral gave me a sense of closure and made me feel connected to my Bubbie as she transitioned out of the physical world. And, throughout my grieving process, I allowed my real feelings to surface whenever they came up. I didn't mask them. I cried when I needed to. I laughed when I thought of my many funny memories with Bubbie. I didn't judge my grieving process. And all of this enabled me to reach the point of acceptance.

Because I'd thoroughly prepared myself (as much as I could, of course), and I'd taken the steps I knew that I'd look back on and be proud of, I was able to accept the reality. And the reality is that Bubbie is no longer here on Earth with me, physically. She doesn't live down the street in assisted living. I can't drive five minutes down the road to see her. I can't call her and hear her cute little voice on the other end of the line. When I'm sad about something, she's not going to be there to talk about it. She won't be able to read this book, the one she always told me I'd write. And although I wish she could be here forever, I know that that was never possible. So I have chosen to accept it. Acceptance is a choice. And it's a choice that is essential to make in order to move forward with your life.

Something we often struggle to accept is that not everyone is built the way we are. And I mean built in terms of the way that we think, how we cope with our feelings, and the way in which we look at the world. We are consistently let down when people don't treat us how we treat them. Why are we always so disappointed? Well, because we're not accepting the fundamental truth that we're not all the same. And we're not supposed to be. We struggle to accept that people are far more emotionally complex than we expect or want them to be. We struggle to accept the fact that we need to take these differences into account in our interactions with others. We need to stop blindly reacting to everyone in the same way, repeatedly.

Another truth we struggle to accept is that life's not fair. And we continue to fight against this fact relentlessly, even though we know intellectually that it's true. Life was never going to be "fair." If you find yourself dwelling on this notion of "fairness" and "justice," take a look at what you might be avoiding in doing so. It's uncomfortable to sit with, right? That we won't always get the justice we deserve. That bad things happen to good people. *But they do.* We need to accept these facts to stay sane and psychologically grounded. We cannot keep driving ourselves crazy thinking things are going to turn out differently or that people are going to change just because we want them to. We need to find meaning in the way that things do turn out, so that we can accept it and move forward into our new realities.

We need to accept that we *don't* have the power to make others like us—and we shouldn't want that power. Because if we're making or forcing others to like us, then it's not unconditional love. It's transactional. Unconditional love is not based on anything outside of that love itself. It doesn't change from season to season. We need to give up our illusion of control over the relationships in our lives. We need to show up as ourselves and allow others the opportunity and freedom to meet us where we *actually are.* We need to accept that being loved and respected and valued in this world comes with—and only with—letting go of our false pretenses and stepping fully into our true selves. We need to let go of the pride. We need to drop the ego and the masks. We need to accept that we don't have nearly as much control as we believe we do. And that's *okay.* And it's freeing.

We need to accept that once we know something about a person or a relationship, we cannot simply unknow it. Once you learn your place in someone's life, you ought to take that in and act accordingly. And it's a difficult thing to do, of course. When you have pure, solid intentions, it's hard to reconfigure what someone means to you and how much effort to put in moving forward. But when we hold onto our delusions and refuse to take in what's right in front of us or within us, we prolong our suffering. You can't rush acceptance, but at a certain point, it must come. If you want to move on, that is. So much of our suffering comes from gripping in vain onto what *was* because we're afraid of change. Acceptance usually brings change. Change to your reality, if nothing else. Again, we need to trust the process. The process driven by our intuition.

If you have trouble with acceptance, take a look at how you define the term. Acceptance doesn't require you to stay in the relationship or to let the other person know they are "off the hook." It doesn't mean that you are weak or that you've failed. Not in the slightest. You can accept from afar. You can make the conscious choice to accept what is in front of you because you know that hanging onto the fantasy is causing you more pain than letting it go. Once you've accepted something, you have the opportunity to move forward how you like. In other words, what comes *after* the acceptance is up to you. But acceptance is a key part of the process.

It's hard to accept something if we don't know what we're holding onto. So, let's think about what that is. Is it the perception that you have of a person? Perhaps someone you highly respect has let you down. And maybe it's difficult for you to view this person in any other way than as a role model. The pre-conceived ideas you have about someone may be preventing you from accepting them *as they are*. If you're not accepting of what is, then you're holding onto a relationship that perhaps is no longer what it was. In other words, you're hanging onto an illusion. You might be struggling to let go of the illusion of control, or the idea that you have the power to keep a relationship going just out of pure will. But not all relationships are meant to be life-long. And when we try and control the quality or direction of a relationship, then we're not even existing in the relationship as it is. We're living in our mental construct of what we want it to be.

You could be keeping yourself in relationships you've outgrown because you're afraid to grow or to let go. Acceptance usually means letting go, whether that's of the perception you have of someone or the someone themselves. Maybe you're letting go of what was, or of a dream you once had about how things could be. The sooner you can accept, the sooner you step into reality. You're no longer operating out of fear and ego. Instead, you're opening up your heart and mind to the present. You're responding to what's *actually happening*, not what you imagine it to be.

We need to accept that not everyone is going to understand us or see us for who we are. We need to accept the fact that there will be people who will have narratives about us that don't match up with our own. We need to accept that people will talk about us and make us fit into whatever context fits the story as they see it. Accept it because it's the reality. And you're here to live in reality, not to fight against it with white knuckles. Accept yourself and your loved ones in full, as well. We need to hold more space for one another as we are, as our natural selves. Acceptance means you're opening up to the here and now. It means you're here, and you have choices as to how to move forward.

Now that I've accepted that my Bubbie is no longer physically present, I can wholeheartedly move forward. I've got years' worth of meaningful memories of her that I can revisit whenever I'm missing her. I feel immense gratitude for all of the many important moments in my life that she was present for. I have no regrets or doubts when it comes to the relationship I had with her. I'm so thankful that I prepared myself, and that my mom prepared me, for the inevitable. My grieving journey would have looked very different had I not been as prepared as I was. It would have looked very different if I didn't welcome the acceptance as a natural part of the process.

Acceptance truly is a gift. It's a gift that you give to yourself. It's permission to move forward. It's permission to feel. It's permission to let go. Acceptance is the point at which you say goodbye to the cycle that kept you in pain. Acceptance means seeing things for what they are in their truest form. It begins by accepting ourselves. All of ourselves. From the inside out. It's accepting that we don't have control over others (nor should we want to). It's accepting what has happened instead of trying to change it or pretend it happened another way. It's living in reality and seeing it for what it is so that you can engage with all that life has to offer. Again, happiness lives here in the present. Oh, the beauty of acceptance! On the other side of it lives the freedom you've been searching for.

Caged within the confines
Of our insecurities we sprawl
Our limiting beliefs in permanent
Ink along the wall and then
We meet these words every day
As soon as the light streams in
And before we are even truly awake
We're reminded of them

And when we wonder why
The light outside our cage
Burns brighter than the one within
We have only to look at the words
We've etched upon the inner corners
Of our mind's eye and realize
We are still clutching the pen.

The Truth Teller

CHAPTER 21

THE TRUTH ABOUT FREEDOM

"A deeper understanding of your consciousness offers you greater freedom in your human experience."
—*Delta Venus (@delta__venus)*

L et's talk about a different kind of freedom. The freedom from within. The land of the free, right? We don't live there. If freedom means mincing our words and restricting ourselves and artificially altering our lives for public consumption, we need a new definition of freedom. Truth is, you're not free if you're hiding from your true self. You're not free if you're living a lie. You're not free if your inner child is still locked inside of you and you're doing whatever you can to ignore her. You're not free if you're wearing a figurative mask. *That's not freedom.*

So, in a world where many of us aren't *externally* free, we need to search for more subtle, creative ways that we can free ourselves in our daily lives. Here are some of the ways I've freed myself: I've freed myself from my eating disorder. I've freed myself from relationships that were no longer serving me. I've freed myself from blindly following the crowd and taking what the crowd says at face value. I've freed myself from the labels that others have tried to cast onto me when they don't like what I'm doing or saying. I've freed myself from limiting beliefs that were never mine to begin with.

And in freeing myself in these ways, I've stepped into myself. I've embodied the truth of who I am and what my life is all about. And I'm able to be present and to fully enjoy it. I couldn't have enjoyed anything if I were holding onto the past or allowing the projections of others to become limiting beliefs that kept me confined. I've given myself permission to free myself from things that I know, deep down, haven't served me. And we can all free ourselves in these ways. But first, we must become aware of what we need to free ourselves from.

Truthfully, most of us don't know what is standing in the way of ourselves and our freedom. Sometimes, it's not anything *external* that inhibits our freedom. It's ourselves. It's the lack of inner work we're doing, and keeping ourselves in unwanted, unhealthy cycles, that is restricting us. Sometimes it's our fear of failure. Or, conversely, it's our fear of our own potential. We may fear that if we go after our goals, then others may abandon us due to their jealousy or differing beliefs. Maybe you were taught that to go after your own dreams, and to put those dreams first, is selfish. But maybe you were taught this from people who haven't ever pursued their *own* dreams. And are these people the best sources of guidance on going after your goals?

Maybe we need to free ourselves, when possible, from the external authority figures that we routinely turn to in times of distress. Perhaps our love for these individuals, or our fear of abandonment, prevents us from seeing that these authority figures are not our best source of guidance. Maybe these authority figures are our own family members or friends. If you're listening continually to these people and their advice doesn't speak to you, or your intuition is screaming at you to go in a different direction, then perhaps it's time to reevaluate your blind allegiance to the guidance provided by these individuals. And sometimes, this means reevaluating your blind allegiance to these individuals themselves. Then who do you turn to? Yourself. Your internal sense of guidance. Your gut instinct.

Now, how do we go about freeing ourselves when we realize it's in our best interest to do so? Social media will present you with a bunch of options. Go on a vacation. Get this new beauty procedure—it'll make you feel like a whole new person! But it doesn't, and it can't. Escape isn't freedom. Changing your appearance won't magically bring about a new you. Keeping your calendar overflowing with plans is only allowing you to temporarily escape your reality. You can't avoid the issue that's holding you back and expect to free yourself from it.

To free ourselves, we must go back to the beginning of this book. We must tune out all the external noise and get quiet with ourselves. We must build our foundation, which includes our value system. We must take off our masks and stare deeply into our own reflections. To free ourselves, we must locate our inner voice.

It is the coming back to our truth, and living in that truth every day, that gives us freedom.

When we give ourselves that permission slip to live our lives authentically, there is nothing holding us hostage. We can go after our dreams without shame. We can let go of those limiting beliefs, both from ourselves and from society, that hold us back. We are free to become the people who we are meant to be.

True freedom comes from letting go of all the societal contradictions we've been conditioned to believe. That we should be confident, but that it's cocky to express that confidence to the world (more on this in the next chapter). That our voice matters, but that we shouldn't use it if we have something contradictory to say. That we should do whatever we can to be "nice" to others, even when that comes at the expense of being kind to ourselves. Freedom starts with the awareness that we are not free, and that we deserve to be.

I feel most free when I am living my life authentically. I am free when I speak up about the things that matter to me. I feel free when I give myself permission to set boundaries in relationships that aren't serving me. I free myself when I put my own needs before those of others (when possible, of course. If you're a parent, there are times this won't be possible. But this is where you must get creative and figure out when and where you can make time for what serves you. After all, you can't pour from an empty cup). I am free when I allow myself to acknowledge and to express the full range of my emotions. I am free when I accept what is instead of fighting against reality. I am free when I allow myself to be. I'm free when I set my fears aside and focus on what I know to be true. And no one can take that away from me. The same goes for you.

Freedom is giving yourself permission to say, "you know what? I see things for what they are. I'm no longer going to stay quiet about the things that matter to me. I will no longer run from what sets my soul on fire. I will respect myself enough not to keep myself in situations where I'm disrespected. I know my worth and my value. I don't want to live my life asleep at the wheel. I'm not here to play it safe. I won't spend my time here on earth apologizing for the things that I know and love about myself. I'm here to be my authentic self. I don't want to simply exist—I want to thrive. And I give myself permission to live in my fullest expression."

The truth is that a vast majority of people who live under oppressive systems around the world aren't free. But there also exists freedom on the micro level, on the individual level. You can choose to speak up, you can choose to walk away, you can choose your values, and you can choose yourself. And until more and more of us—as individuals—start making the choice to free ourselves in our own daily lives, we won't have the capacity to go after the broader-scale changes that need to be made in our world. We need to begin somewhere. It's a journey, and it's a choice to take that journey. No one is telling you that it's going to be easy. It's not. It's the hardest fucking thing you will ever set your mind to. But it's also *the* most important, healthy, productive, meaningful, beautiful type of work you can do. The land of the free? Not quite. Freedom of the self? Absolutely.

She was taught to sit pretty
Arms delicately placed over
Crossed legs adorned in
Tights that swallowed all the contours
Right out of her, but they looked nice
Or so they said.

She thought so, too,
But when she said the words aloud
Somehow all the beauty was sucked
Right out of her grasp by their beady eyes
Admonishing her for uttering the words
They all were thinking already
For she wasn't supposed to speak them
But just to sit pretty, after all.

The Truth Teller

CHAPTER 21

THE TRUTH ABOUT
CONFIDENCE

*"We beg women to love themselves but tell
confident women to calm down."*
— *Tyra B. Laster*

I t's hard to feel true freedom if you're not confident in yourself. You can hop on whatever train or jet plane you want,
but you'll still be the same passenger. So, buckle up. This
is going to be quite a chapter. Because the question most frequently asked of me, whether online or IRL, is how I am so
confident. When I'm asked to describe myself in a few words,
confidence is always right at the top. When my loved ones are
asked to describe me, confidence is also one of the very first
words they mention. It's always been that way. I can genuinely
say that I'm confident, inside and out. I love myself, and I'm not
afraid to say that. And, hey, I can already guess what some of
you are thinking. That I must be full of myself. That I'm cocky
to even be saying any of this. *As if we don't tell women to love themselves proudly.* Our society confuses confidence with cockiness,
and we don't know where to draw the line. And since we aren't
clear on what confidence truly looks like anymore, we don't
know how to receive those who proudly express their confidence to the world.

And why do so many of us not know what confidence truly
looks like? Well, because we live in a world that *preaches* self-
love, but at the same time, judges the shit out of those who love
themselves proudly. Our society will talk out of one side of its
mouth about being true to yourself and the value of confidence,

but in the same breath it'll shame you for actually *expressing* that confidence. The messages are endlessly convoluted and contradictory. "Love yourself, but not in a way that's over the top." "Be confident, but don't really *show* it because then you'll be perceived as 'cocky.'" "Embrace your natural beauty, but you should also get this new plastic surgery procedure that everyone is getting—it's non-invasive!" It's exhausting and maddening, and frankly, it makes no sense. The truth is this: society likes to *say* it stands for women loving themselves and it likes to *preach* about the importance of women being confident, but when it comes down to it, our society is scared as shit of confident women.

When young, we're taught to embrace our natural beauty and all that makes us unique. We get a little older and we learn the importance of using positive affirmations and practicing self-love. But then we look around and we see how society *treats* confident people (and, yes, I am primarily focusing on confident *women* here, since we're dealing with an arsenal of double standards when it comes to female confidence). We don't always treat them with respect. We often act as though we do not "like" them. We mock them and tear them down. We make them feel *bad* about feeling *good*. We make them question themselves and see if we can introduce them to a little insecurity so they will be less of a threat to us. We gossip and judge them relentlessly.

But let me tell you a little something about judgment. (Shoutout to my amazing business partner, Camilla, for teaching me this!) The purpose of judgment is to create distance. We judge who or what makes us uncomfortable to try and separate ourselves from the uncomfortable feeling that person inspires in us. Maybe we feel threatened or insecure around this person, so instead of getting *curious* about *why* that is, we judge them. If we just label the person as cocky, self-centered, or rude, then we don't have to get real with ourselves about *why* we feel this sense of unease around them. You can't be curious while judging. Curiosity and judgment cannot possibly coexist because when you judge someone, you've already determined how you feel about them. But, if you get curious, you just might be able to be honest with yourself about your own insecurities and why you feel the way you do. And the way you feel around this person has far more to do with you than it does that other person. It's not *their* fault you feel the way you do. *They* are not the problem. But, as a society, we have *made* them out to be the problem because most people don't know how to get honest about their *own* problems.

As a confident woman myself, I've been questioned throughout my life about my motivations when I express said confidence. It's not seen as "relatable" to talk about what you love about yourself. If you put yourself out there, you'll get praise on one side of the coin and shame on the other. If you're feeling good about yourself and post a picture on your Instagram, you're opening yourself up to the judgments about you being "desperate" and "needing validation" instead of people realizing that we can post images of ourselves simply because we feel confident enough to do so. We don't leave room for the simple truth that some people *do* just love themselves and are proud to express it. And when we don't make space for this truth, we dissuade others from joining the confidence club. Because who wants to be called conceited?

So, let's talk about the difference between cockiness and confidence, since we obviously keep getting the two confused. Cockiness is *needing* external validation because you don't feel an inner sense of self-worth. This means that when external praise goes away, so too does the over-inflated sense of self. Confidence, on the other hand, lives within. A confident person looks and feels confident across the board because their sense of worth is not dependent on their external environment. Cockiness is not being able to admit to any flaws or wrongdoings. It's never being able to see a need to work on the self because the cocky person thinks they have it all figured out. Confident people often understand that learning and self-development is a lifelong process; they're able and willing to take a deeper look under their own hood. Cockiness rests on the opinions of others; confidence does not.

The truth is that I've always been confident. Even from a young age, I'd parade around the house and in public singing and dancing for all to see and listen. I'd walk up to literal strangers and introduce myself and strike up a conversation. I could always tell you exactly what I loved about myself. Just ask. I'm extremely comfortable in front of a camera, on a stage, or in the mirror. So yes, I'm naturally confident. However! The key to confidence is trusting yourself. I've built on my confidence over the years by trusting my instincts when they arise and following these instincts on whatever path they take me. I put myself out there and watch myself rise to the occasion whenever I do. I give myself an opportunity to step up to the plate. This is key. Furthermore, confidence comes from knowing yourself, flaws and all. When you can acknowledge and embrace both your strengths and weaknesses, you can become a confident individual. This, of course, goes back to doing the work. The more self-aware you are, the less you're affected by what others think or say about you. Because you know yourself. You know what belongs to you and what doesn't.

I also never join in on those group conversations where everyone is ragging on themselves, because I'm not going to join in on the self-deprecation just to feel like I fit in. I express my opinion, even if it differs from that of the crowd. And yes, this has sometimes gotten me the raised eyebrows. But I'm not going to pick myself apart performatively just so that I can join the insecurity club. Because I do believe that what we tell ourselves shapes our reality. I've spoken to many people as a therapist and in my personal life that struggle with self-confidence. And one commonality I've noticed amongst these individuals is that they don't open themselves up to even the mere *possibility* of confidence. They've decided very emphatically and matter-of-factly that they're just *never* going to be confident. Period. End of story. But that's a choice. Just because you've never been confident doesn't mean you can't ever be. You don't have to look a certain way to be confident. You don't have to have any specific traits to be confident, either. You just need to have a willingness to find the pieces of yourself that you love and are proud of. And you need to find the courage to love these things, even if no one else around you is praising you for this self-love.

Now, I'm not saying that it's easy or simple to become a confident individual. But what I'm asking you is to be honest with yourself about whether or not you've closed yourself off entirely to the idea. How do you, personally, feel about confident people? What are your limiting beliefs around confidence? Are you doing anything to work on increasing your self-confidence? If not, why not? Confidence is something to work towards. The more you practice it, the more it naturally comes to you. If you never put yourself out there, how can you expect to feel any differently about yourself? Confidence requires trust and faith in yourself. It also requires a lot of inner strength. Because, yes, you might be judged. But you're going to be judged no matter what, so why not be judged for loving yourself proudly?

Isn't this what we, as a society, try and preach, anyway? *Let's look in the mirror and speak positively to ourselves. Let's be proud of our natural selves.*

How are we supposed to be proud of our natural selves if we're shamed whenever we get in touch with and express that natural self?

Maybe if we embrace what we are personally confident about in public, we can create a safe space for others to do the same. And if you don't understand the importance of embracing our confidence publicly, get real about why that is. Be careful about labeling someone a narcissist (a word some people throw around without any sense of the true definition) when you see them posing for pictures or saying something about themselves that they love. It's easier to write people off as cocky (and try to diminish their confidence by making a mockery of them in an attempt to somehow feel better about ourselves) than it is to sit with the icky feelings that we might get around those who hold their head up high. And we need to start to get it through our collective consciousness that it is *possible and realistic* to be confident without any negative connotation. Being confident is something to be *proud* of, no apologies.

As someone who helps others for a living, a large part of my day is focusing on *other* people and helping them with *their* problems. But I do love myself, and—quite frankly—I couldn't help anyone else or even be truly compassionate toward them if I wasn't that way towards myself first and foremost. And we should feel *proud*, not ashamed, to say that we love ourselves fiercely. I am proud that my confidence inspires more confidence around me. I understand that my confidence is polarizing: you'll either be able to get with it, or you will not know how to tolerate it (which, truthfully, tells me a heck of a lot about the other person and how they feel about themselves). And in turn, it makes it pretty easy to figure out who is meant to be in my life and who is not. The truth is, if you try and make someone feel bad about their confidence, you're telling them that they can never allow their true self to shine through around you without apologizing for it in some way. Conversely, confidence invites more confidence. If you surround yourself with those who are unafraid to speak positively about themselves, you may be encouraged to do it, too. And if you surround yourself with people who constantly put themselves down, well, what are you inviting into your life?

I know what it takes to be confident in our world. It's no easy feat to hold onto our childhood confidence in a society where we are taught that picking ourselves apart makes us "relatable" and "cool." Well, let me tell you something: it's not "cool" to pick ourselves apart. It's disrespectful to ourselves and those around us to scrutinize ourselves in this way, and it doesn't get us anywhere. When someone tries to shame you for being confident, it's often rooted in their own insecurities. It comes from people who don't love themselves. It comes from those who were taught to be ashamed of loving themselves, probably from others who were taught the same thing. And is this really the message we want to be passing down from generation to generation?

Would you rather live a life where you can walk around feeling the pride and freedom of complete self-confidence, even if it means you might walk without some people, than hold yourself back to be with those who don't love themselves? Listen, the choice is ultimately yours. And many people choose the latter because it's a safer, easier option. It's just not the happiest option. It's not the option that will lead you to live your healthiest, truest existence. Many people, or most, won't choose the former because it takes a lot of inner strength and courage. So, if you know a confident person, remember this: they have remained confident *in spite* of being unfairly criticized, shamed, or ostracized by our insecure world. And *that* is true self-love right there.

So, I have a proposition for us: let's normalize talking highly about ourselves. Gone are the days when picking ourselves apart and finding flaws as a way of connecting with others can be portrayed as "cool" (yes, if you thought of Mean Girls and the scene with Regina George and clan standing in front of a full-length mirror picking themselves apart and then looking at Cady expectantly to join in, you know what I mean). Let's start talking about what we love about ourselves. At first, it will feel weird, especially if you're not used to it. Confidence does not come naturally to everyone, but it's something you can practice and begin to teach yourself. Take note of who you surround yourself with, as misery loves company, and this is often the case with insecure people. If you're around confident people, well, chances are you will begin to adopt some of the traits of a confident person. You'll observe the way they act and how they speak about themselves. And you'll be inspired to find that confidence within—that is, if you're not focused on judging them.

The truth is that, until we can *allow* ourselves to be confident without inflicting shame on one another for it, we cannot live out our true essence. As children, a lot of us were confident! And, of course, living out your truth means coming back to your inner child because that is the core of your being. So, what happened to all of those confident children? We need to find them and bring them to light. And one way we can accomplish this is by those of us who are confident showing our confidence in a way that invites others to do the same. If we're all constantly speaking negatively about ourselves and judging others for being confident, how can we expect anyone to strive for self-confidence?

The reality is thus: a confident person should not offend you. They should inspire you. The confident woman is a living example of strength and self-worth that shines from the inside out. The confidence, itself, is not the problem. The problem is that we are *making* that the problem. The problem is that society doesn't know how to properly respect confident people—namely women. It preaches messages that it can't actually stand by. Listen, if we're going to tell people to love themselves, then don't be surprised when they do! Also, try loving yourself sometime. Truth be told, you're better off putting all that energy you're using to judge others for being confident into working on loving yourself more.

Truth is, you're a wannabe
Nothing new here to see
You bought it on a shopping spree
Right after you saw it on me
Copying isn't free
Originality is key
Find someone who will disagree
You won't, I guarantee
Clearly, you're a newbie
Taking notes from the queen bee
Barking up my damn tree
That'll cost you a pretty penny
Acting like it's easy breezy
When really, it's just cheesy
Let me put it to you bluntly
What you lack is authenticity.

The Truth Teller

CHAPTER 22

THE TRUTH ABOUT
AUTHENTICITY

"Authenticity equals longevity."
— Lanna Monday Emmett
(@lanna_Monday_emmett)

Want to know the real key to anti-aging? It's not the latest moisturizer you saw on TikTok last week or the $17.00 smoothie a celebrity put out the other day. Yes, genes and lifestyle play a role. Yes, skincare and what you put inside your body are certainly part of it. But the key that we are missing? It's authenticity. Authenticity leads to longevity. Those who are youthful and who embody youth from the inside out are, most likely, living their lives authentically. Do you want to live long and radiate from the inside out? You won't get there without being true to yourself.

So, first, let's talk about what it means to be authentic. Authenticity is being who you were meant to be. It's about living from a place of ultimate truth within yourself. It's about living in accordance with your values and being honest. It's about taking ownership and accountability of yourself. It's about seeing yourself for who you are, at your true essence, and loving that person, unconditionally. It's doing the same for those around you. It's being original. Because we are all, fundamentally, original. It's being genuine in your relationships and in your interactions with others. It's turning to your own inner child for guidance. It's forging your own, unique path that speaks to who you are as an individual.

Living authentically has always been extremely important to me. Perhaps one of the earliest memories I have of being authentic is in third grade. We had a parent day where all the parents came to class and each student had to come up with a special activity to present to them. Each kid would stand behind their own table ready to present the activity they'd chosen while the parents and other students would walk around to the different stations. Well, I was thrilled by this assignment! I loved to share my hobbies and interests with others from a young age. At the time, I was a tap dancer. It was my favorite form of dance, and I excelled at it. So, I thought for my activity I could teach a few tap steps to whoever came up to my table. I could share my real passion with my peers and hopefully get them excited about trying something new.

Well, the day came, and here I was standing amongst tables with freshly baked cookies and sand art, and I watched as everyone flocked to the tables with the big take-home prizes. Of course, looking back, third graders are going to want to go to the station where they can create some cool art project to bring home or eat something delicious that's smelling up the whole room. Here I was with my dinky little tap-dancing sign, wearing my good ol' tap shoes. And no one was coming up to my table. And I couldn't understand why. After a while, I had one mother come up to me, who clearly felt badly that I was standing alone as I longingly looked at those tables around me with my friends and their parents lined up. I had a teacher come up to me to try and learn my tap steps, as well as one single student, both of whom clearly also felt sad for me as I stood alone. Those were my only three visitors of the day. I remember it vividly to this day, the feeling of sadness, shame, and confusion over why no one came to my table.

When I look back at this core memory, I still feel that pang in my chest for my younger self. But I am so damn proud of her. She always marched to her own beat. I easily could have done whatever would have been popular if I was thinking about the assignment like that. If my goal was to get as many people as possible to come up to my table, well yes, I could have just baked something. But quite honestly, when presented with the assignment, that thought didn't even occur to me. To me, it was about choosing something I was passionate about. No shame to the cookie-bakers, but also, no shame at all that I went in a different direction. One that spoke to me. And I wouldn't change that about myself if I could.

Authenticity isn't easy when you're young, facing peer-pressure, and the potential of standing apart from the crowd. Clearly, the reason that I remember this experience so vividly is because it was quite painful. I could have internalized it and allowed it to make me question myself moving forward. I could have chosen to do whatever was in my power, from then on, to blend in. But, as difficult as it is to stand alone, there's no feeling as powerful as knowing who you are and being proud of that person. I don't think I'd have remembered the experience at all if I was one of the sand art people, but because I was the one who chose to teach others something new and a bit outside the box, I'll always be reminded of my courage and authenticity.

Let's pretend you have the assignment, today, of bringing an activity to the metaphorical table of your peers. Let this be something that speaks to your inner child. Think back to what you enjoyed as a kid. Maybe it was dancing. Maybe it was art. Maybe it was sports. How could you share that passion with others? Now, notice if any fears are popping up. Maybe you're fearing what people might think of what you choose. Or maybe you're second-guessing your activity. Is this something you really loved? Notice the fears in little thought bubbles and attach these thought bubbles to faces of your peers. This way, you can separate yourself from them. Those thoughts don't come from your inner child. You're the expert on yourself. You're the only one who can tell you what it is you truly love and what excites you. Whatever you end up choosing for this pretend assignment, ask yourself if you're still making time for that thing today. If not, why not? Can you start to reintegrate, or make time for, whatever it was? It might be difficult, and you might tell yourself you don't have the time. But when there's a will, there's a way. Find the way.

If you don't make authenticity an optional *choice*, but just a way of *being*, it becomes easier to step into.

If you quit looking for your answers outside of yourself, you'll only be left with the ones within.

And yes, there is a difference between being authentic and using authenticity as a permission slip to be a completely unfiltered asshole. There is a way in which to tactfully frame things in certain contexts of your life. But that doesn't mean that you still can't always be coming from a place of your truth and not compromising who it is that you are at your core. Authenticity involves integrity. It's living and acting from a place of alignment with your values and who you are: yes, that inner child we keep coming back to.

So, what's the link between authenticity and longevity? Well, if you're not honest with yourself, you may not notice those physical ailments you might be having. Maybe you're so cut off from yourself that you ignore them completely. You don't go to the doctor because you're living in your delusion that everything is fine and dandy. This is the danger of being disconnected from yourself. And then your health worsens until you can no longer ignore your symptoms. And then your overall health is impacted, maybe beyond repair. See, when you're honest with yourself and those around you, and when you're aware of what you might be struggling with, you can address these issues early on. You have the awareness and wherewithal to deal with whatever comes up.

The other link between authenticity and longevity is that if you're not allowing yourself to feel and express your emotions, they'll get stuck inside of you and begin to fester. Your unresolved psychological trauma can turn into physical ailments (this process is called somatization). If you're holding onto unexpressed anger, for example, this anger might show up as tension in your body. That tension can grow and grow until it becomes a bigger and more severe physical ailment. Or maybe you have so much unreleased and unprocessed anxiety that your heart begins to beat irregularly. You see where this is going. When you don't allow your emotions to move through you, you're just trapping them inside of you until they explode into something unmanageable and seriously problematic. Authenticity allows you to have a better outcome. Then you have a clean, healthy inside that translates to your outer self. Fuck that new diet. Authenticity is what works wonders.

Living an authentic life is less stressful than wearing a mask. Think about it. When you're free to say what you mean and aren't holding things back, your mind and body are more at ease. As an authentic person, I can tell you that it's fucking relaxing. Because there is no "figuring out" how to be. You're just being you. You're not morphing into a different persona around other people. You don't have to modify yourself based on the crowd you're around. There aren't different versions of you around different people in your life. All of your different crews could be in one room and you wouldn't have to worry about how to be. And when you're just you, you are attuned to your unique needs, which you can then address. You know that just because this celebrity is on this new diet, that that wouldn't necessarily work for you based on your own history. You're aware enough to know how much sleep your body needs, so you give it the appropriate rest. You make decisions based on true knowledge about what is best for *you*. This is exactly why health and authenticity go hand in hand. People who are in tune with themselves and their internal states are more likely to live in accordance with their internal state's needs.

Authenticity isn't only essential for you as an individual; it's also important for every relationship in your life. People trust those who are authentic because they know they're being honest. People will seek you out when they want the hard truth. You can form deeper relationships with others when you're being your whole self. Others are more inclined to be authentic with you when you yourself are coming from a place of authenticity. When you're authentic, you can trust that your decisions are coming from the right place. And even if some choices are difficult to make, you will ultimately have the peace of mind that your decision is what is best for you. Conversely, if you're always looking outside of yourself for the answers, you'll always be left wondering if you would have been better off trusting your gut.

Finally, if you want to have any sort of impact in the world, whether big or small, you will need to come from a place of authenticity. Otherwise, you're not bringing anything new to the table. You're not adding value, you're just adding more of the same. You're not inspiring others to follow their own instincts. You're just encouraging others to play it safe and follow the crowd. Authenticity is freeing, all-encompassing, and is truly what leads to living a full, vibrant life. Authenticity is that connection to your inner child, which is the link to your youth. Quit looking in the skincare aisle and look within.

They're peering into the foggy window
Steeped in snow, trying to catch a glimpse
Of her, this creature who sits curled up
With nothing but a blanket and her journal
They try and make sense of the way she sits
With such poise and elegance
Seemingly unbothered by the chaotic snowfall
That's wreaking havoc just outside the walls
She's always been lightyears ahead
Constantly uncovering a constellation
Of epiphanies and digging deep
Into the endless layers of her soul
Where the wisdom and the youth intertwine
Into the expansive mural of her identity
They want to see if there's a trick to this
A potion they can sip
They don't understand that the magic
Cannot be simply witnessed
That the real peace lives within themselves
And that's the only way it can be experienced.

The Truth Teller

CHAPTER 23

THE TRUTH ABOUT
IDENTITY

"If your identity is a place, a style, a feeling, or another person—you don't have one."
— *The Truth Teller (aka @thattrendytherapist)*

'm a firm believer that there is no work more important than the work on the self. We obviously have a plethora of issues that exist within society. But if we start at the basis of our society, which is comprised of us individuals, it becomes clearer why we are collectively struggling. At an individual level, we are deeply hurting. This fact became undeniably obvious throughout the pandemic. Often, when there's an upheaval or crisis, there are underlying issues—that had previously been hidden and out of our awareness—that rise to the surface. The collective trauma of the pandemic triggered us all in our own ways. But one commonality is that it forced us all inward. It left us with no choice but to take a look under the rug at the issues we'd swept under there. We had to take an honest look at ourselves in the mirror and discover if we liked what we saw.

And many of us didn't. And we fell into a state of despair. The rates of depression and suicide skyrocketed, as did the number of people seeking therapy for the first time. People are hurting. And during the pandemic, they could no longer escape the fact that they were fundamentally unhappy. That, when they were forced to stop and look at their bare-faced reflection without their mask on (both the literal and figurative ones), they couldn't meet their own eyes. And we need to quit pretending like this *isn't* our reality. We need to stop telling people to just "be positive!"— as if that's going to magically change anything. We need to stop acting like going to the gym six days a week and drinking celery juice will solve our underlying problems. We need to think deeper. And we need to do it quickly.

Because we see the trends. And say what you will about trends, but trends don't lie. There's a reason certain things become popular at any given time, and those things are a direct reflection of where we are at as a society. It's no coincidence that what's currently trendy is to discuss our mental health. You can now scroll through Tik-Tok and see videos of people openly discussing their mental health issues and ways they're dealing with these issues. As a therapist, I'm thrilled that mental health is finally getting the spotlight it so deserves and desperately needs. We've been needing to speak about mental health since yesterday. But, also, this newfound discussion surrounding mental health includes people doling out advice when they aren't qualified to do so. And, oftentimes, this advice is insanely problematic.

We've now got pre-teens diagnosing themselves with mental disorders after seeing a thirty-second TikTok video. We have a plethora of advice at our fingertips about what we can do when we don't know which way to turn. And, sometimes, this advice is helpful. But sometimes, there's so much of it to parse through that it leaves us feeling more confused. If we're already feeling lost, and someone is boasting about how this new strategy or way of existing in the world has transformed their life, we are susceptible to following said advice (because, of course, we just want to feel better). And I want to say this here and now: many, many individuals *do* have mental health disorders. There is nothing illegitimate about that fact. But we must not forget that there are certain diagnostic criteria that one has to meet in order to be properly diagnosed with these types of mental illnesses. The same ones that thirteen-year-olds are self-diagnosing themselves with from the internet. And while there's some really great advice out there, spoken by professionals or others from their own personal experience, we're also inundated with information that isn't helpful, might not pertain to us, and could potentially be dangerous.

Few want to talk about the problematic nature of self-diagnosing because it's entirely controversial. There are endless ways to spin it, and there are many people who will find a way to do so. It's often challenging to discern whether this new-found identity of many of today's youth is coming from a place of authenticity or is just a mask they're wearing to fit in.

What we can and should agree on is that this rise in self-diagnosing is happening not only because of the rise in conversation surrounding mental health, but because we have a collective identity crisis.

People don't know who they are, and they're searching desperately for the answers in all the wrong places. And what's ultimately happening is that more and more human beings are making drastic, sudden, and sometimes irreversible decisions in their lives because a certain identity seems attractive to them in the moment, but later reveals itself to only have been a stand-in for their true identity.

It's not our fault. When we don't know who we are and we're constantly bombarded with different identities we can try on like prom dresses, why wouldn't we? We're trying to figure ourselves out. And yes, oftentimes figuring ourselves out includes trying on different metaphorical hats to see what fits.

But what if we shift the focus internally? What if the answers about who we are don't come from that smiling influencer, swearing that the key to health and happiness is embedded in this new medication they tried last week? What if they aren't *actually* happy and you're mistaking their enthusiasm for the answers to all of life's suffering? Sometimes we do end up stumbling upon someone who changes our paths completely and helps us realize something about ourselves that we'd been previously blind to. But the truth is, most of the time we can find out who we truly are just by diving deeper into ourselves.

There was a time, as I've said, that I lost sight of who I was. When I had my eating disorder, I was grasping onto the identity of being "the smallest one." But what was the significance of being the smallest person in my friend group? Yes, I could fit in a certain size of jeans, but this identity lacked any real meaning to me as an individual. It didn't make me feel whole. It was just a temporary mask I wore at a time in my life where I'd lost sight of myself. It didn't make me feel fulfilled. I felt empty inside. I was lost. In my recovery, when I revisited my inner child for answers, I was able to shed the place-holder identity of "the smallest one" and come back to my true self.

When you don't do this self-work, you're in danger of attaching to external sources to fill you with what you're lacking internally. You might look for a sense of wholeness or security in a relationship. If you don't enter into a romantic relationship, for example, without at least some sense of self, you're at risk of losing yourself in the relationship completely. If you're not personally developed, you'll be likely to gravitate toward someone who fills that void. Oftentimes, this person has the qualities that you lack. They might be controlling. They might begin to tell you what to do, say, wear, and eat, because they know that they can have this power over you. And then, you start to lose sight of what's coming from you and what isn't. You get brainwashed. You internalize what your partner is saying and confuse it as your own truth. And it's easy to do this when you don't know your own truth. This is how co-dependent, and many other forms of toxic relationships, form.

If you don't have a sense of self, you might look for it in a physical location. Maybe you've always dreamed of living in Paris. You romanticize Paris because it seems like everyone there, from the movies you've watched to the images you see on social media, is truly happy. So, you move to Paris. You think it's going to fill you with all those missing pieces you can't seem to locate within yourself. And six months down the line, after the newness of the move is over, you are left wondering why you don't feel any different. You still don't feel whole. You're not more self-assured. You can't be more self-assured within yourself by picking up and moving to another state or country. You can't gain a sense of self through any destination or relationship outside of yourself. You are you, wherever you go. Or, in other words, wherever you go, there you are.

We sleep on this self-work, or the discovery of our true identities, because we're never taught how important knowing ourselves really is. There is no class in school that teaches self-love. Instead, we're bombarded with external templates of identities and strategies from others which become appealing when we can't find our own. So, we try them on. Maybe I'll try "emo" today. Maybe I'm a "free-spirit" tomorrow. Maybe if I hang out with the popular group, I'll feel relevant. We try these identities on for size, one by one, hoping desperately that one will feel "just right." But they never do, and we continue to bounce around from one to the next until we've lost sight of our true selves completely. And of course, finding ourselves sometimes requires trial and error. But maybe we're looking for ourselves in the wrong place. Perhaps our inner truth knows more about who we are than a group of people at your school or on social media.

Well, since most of us have never learned the importance of discovering our unique identity, let's talk about why it's important. If you don't know how to define yourself, then you won't have a sense of your purpose. Your purpose in life, the reason that you're here, stems from this identity. It's your innate characteristics, the strengths you've been given that set you apart, that reveal what we are meant to do here on Earth. Knowing ourselves helps us differentiate our feelings from those of others. If you can't tell how you feel separate and apart from those around you, you won't be able to vocalize those feelings. Or to properly cope with them. When you know who you are, you can begin to work on the self-love part. But you can't love yourself if you don't know yourself. And happiness? You can't be truly happy if you don't have that self-love.

In my recovery from my eating disorder, it was time to come back to myself and reconnect with that inner child I'd buried deep within. She was there, reminding me that we didn't like to be quiet. We liked to express ourselves. We liked to create things and find deeper meaning. We liked to bring beauty to the world. We wanted to share our innate gifts with the world and do so without shame, unapologetically. We are bold and fierce and brave. And when I truly got quiet and started to listen to all this inner knowledge, I understood how to piece myself back together, from the ground up. I had my road map, and I didn't get this roadmap on social media. I sourced it from within.

IDENTITY

The great thing about this self-work is that you can start whenever and wherever you are at along your journey. It's never too late to sit with yourself and discover the parts of you that you've lost along the way. You can always come back to yourself. First, you need to be aware that you're lost. Once you have this awareness, you know it's time to start digging deep. When you know who you are, you have what matters most. You're never lost. You won't need to turn to anything outside of yourself to feel like you matter enough to be here. You won't feel incapable of existing in the world. You'll be able to form that trust within yourself that's essential for going after the life that's meant for you, the one you deserve. The one your inner child deserves. And if you haven't taken the time on your journey thus far to turn inward, and you still don't know who it is that you are and what the fuck you are doing on this planet, drop everything else you are doing until you do that. I promise you, nothing else you are doing is nearly as important. Or productive.

She's got eyes like jawbreakers
Always gaping
Sapphire balls laden with
Constant trepidation
Pleading with you not to perforate
Their transparent, swirling exterior

They swirl at me
Tantalizing me, testing me
They know one crunch between my
Threatening teeth and they'll shatter
Into secrets

Jawbreakers
Pink and green, orange
All of them cradled in a mass in that glass
Back at the mall when I was four
I'd ask mom for one just to see it spiral
Down toward my open palm
And I'd bring it to my mouth for a few sucks
Until it'd inevitably lose its flavor

Those tantalizing sapphire jawbreakers
Tantalizing yet sickening
They repulse me when I think of their
Chewy interior
For they'll never be firm as steel all the way through
Like mine

And they gape atop
That slick, well-trimmed smile
She wears that smile everyday
And yet more days than not I know
There's anguish swimming under it

Those pleading jawbreaker eyes
Plead with me to stick in my quarter
And release their burdensome weight
Of trembling trouble
Into my palm
To clasp them into safety

Although what I'd do if I attained one of them
Just one
Is shake it vigorously
Until the sweat of my palms
Made its sapphire exterior bleed
Tie-dye into my hand
Just like my jawbreakers did when I was four
When I saved them for later

And once my hands were so sticky
That they'd barely be able to un-clench themselves
From her jawbreakers
I'd tear them away from my palm
By my teeth
Sucking and shattering
Until I could taste the rich sugar
Which I already know will run out after a few seconds.

The Truth Teller, written in 2011 at Trinity College

CHAPTER 24

THE TRUTH ABOUT
PEACE

"Peace isn't an experience free of challenges, free of rough and smooth—it's an experience that's expansive enough to include all that arises without feeling threatened."
—Pema Chödrön

A lot of people like to make peace their goal. When asked what they want in life, they say they want to feel at peace. And, at first glance, that sounds nice. But what does that *really* mean? Life is never going to be entirely peaceful if you're actually engaging with it. We are all aware that life has its ups and downs. So, usually, those who cling onto peace as if their lives depend on it are avoiding some aspect of real life. They clutch fiercely onto the sounds of waves or the comforts of food in order to numb themselves from feeling life's natural ebbs and flows. But that's not actually achieving peace. It's just avoiding real life

Real life is not always harmonious. So, in order to achieve peace, the peace-seeker must cut themselves off somehow. They must detach. They fade into the background when a fight erupts in the living room. They may leave the room entirely. Or, conversely, they may become the peace-keeper, and try and keep the peace between parties at all costs. But, as we've discussed, sometimes a situation doesn't call for peace-keeping. Sometimes the two parties need to have it out, because there's a real issue going on that needs to be addressed. This is when chronic peace-keeping becomes toxic. The peacekeepers end up creating the very thing they don't want: conflict. Think about it like this: if you're upset with someone and are in the middle of trying to express your feelings to them and then you have your other friend over there trying to weasel their way into the conversation by saying "just let it go!" you're going to start getting annoyed with the weasel, aren't you?

While conflict can feel scary, it's also necessary. It's a way in which people learn more about one another and themselves. It's a way to go deeper. And that's why peace-seekers and keepers usually end up feeling like they're not seen or heard. They shy away from the important conversations that would *allow for* and *foster* real growth and self-development. If someone is coming to you with an issue they have, and you dismiss them because you just want to feel at peace, then your relationship with that individual is going to suffer. Peace-seekers usually have a difficult time locating themselves, or their own identity. They have no defined sense of self, because having a defined sense of self requires you to stand apart from your environment and have your own opinion. The peace-seeker chronically blends in. Their voice, their existence, loses its significance, simply by their own doing. If you're always just an echo of whatever everyone else is saying, and are never providing your own perspective, then people aren't going to seek you out for guidance.

Those who chronically run toward peace are often deeply afraid to feel. They are those who "zone out" to life. They're NOT woke. They do whatever they can to try and keep a serene mind by blocking out the reality of what is going on around them. And you know what happens? Life continues to go on around you even when you attempt to tune it out—you're just not a part of it because you've closed yourself off. You've removed yourself from being an active participant in your life. Your connections will take a toll. People will become frustrated and angry with you because of your avoidance and your disconnection from your own anger. What you don't deal with becomes a problem for others, and they're left picking up your emotional slack. So you're not that peaceful to be around. You're just creating more of a problem.

What many people miss about peace is that it comes from embracing and engaging with all that life has to offer. It's not the absence of struggle or the avoidance of turbulence that makes someone feel at peace.

If you're always searching for that "zen" feeling, it's probably because you're defining peace as needing a break from real life. You feel a need to escape from your reality. What you're doing is zoning out and disengaging with real life. Because, truth be told, if you were *truly* at peace, you wouldn't need to escape into ten hours of television to restore your equilibrium. You'd be able to feel that peacefulness wherever you are. If you constantly feel like you need an escape, that means you're not truly at peace in your daily life.

The myth about peace is that it's the absence of all "drama." But it's often the people who fight against conflict who have the least internal peace. They're afraid of conflict because they don't believe they can handle it. The truth is that there will *always* be conflict. And it's those who can embrace it and see it as a natural part of life who are truly at peace. All of that inner turmoil and anxiety you get every time there is friction in your environment, and your tendency to shut down and make light of it or to move away from it, is actually *keeping* you in a state of tension. You are disconnected from what is actually going on around you. And you will never be completely at peace that way.

See, clinging onto peace may actually be preventing you from experiencing the natural highs of life. Because the peace-seeker keeps their life static. They may not dip into the depths of "drama" and despair, but you don't see them jumping for joy much, either. They become numb to all feelings that take them away from their comfort zone. You might be mistaking being content for being happy if you've never experienced pure, jolting, electrifying joy before. Of course, we cannot conceptualize something we've never personally experienced. So we don't know that it exists. But when you put in the work, and you're an embodied person who truly loves yourself, then you *do* experience lightning-bolt moments of euphoria. Yes, you will have the moments where you struggle to see the light, but you know it's there and sooner or later, you'll get around to facing it. That is, if you put in the work to release the fear you have around discomfort.

I'm a rather serious person—in general. That is, I take myself seriously. I take my life seriously. I live with intention. This doesn't mean I don't smile, laugh until my stomach aches, dance, and get thrilled and overjoyed. I do, and I let those things happen naturally from a place of authenticity—not in a way that's forced or as a performance to get others to approve of me. Because I attend to my inner child's deepest needs, and don't ignore or invalidate her, when she's feeling joy, she's out to play. My energy is limitless, and people seek it out. They want to know how I've managed to embody my inner child so fully. Well, it's because I pay attention to her, respect her, and make sure I'm meeting her needs. That's how.

When I say that I'm serious about myself and my life, I mean that I love myself and know my worth. I'm not going to sleep on myself and my purpose. But so many of us *do* let our purpose go to waste. In fact, many of us never even learn what our purpose is. At all. We just exist, running through the days and checking things mindlessly off our to-do lists without any overall understanding of our bigger picture. And when you don't take yourself seriously, everything becomes a joke. You unconsciously give yourself the excuse to not put in the real work on yourself and your life. Because you tell yourself it doesn't really matter. You live your life vicariously through others. You live constrained by your own limiting beliefs and your fear of not being significant. Well, you're not going to feel as if your life has any significance if you don't take yourself seriously. That's just the truth.

If you're sleeping on yourself, that's a choice. It's avoidance, fear, insecurity, and a plethora of other issues that you are making the choice not to face. Because, yes, everyone can do the work. Even if you're not going to therapy, you can do the work. If you're not consciously taking the time to work through what holds you back, then don't sit there and wonder why you're not feeling connected or joyous. Joy comes from putting in the work. It comes from knowing who you are, expressing yourself, respecting yourself, and honoring your true feelings. True joy comes from loving yourself. It comes from living out your passions and your purpose. It doesn't come from hiding and avoiding and neglecting and running. You can exist that way, and you can fool yourself into thinking all is well, but perhaps it's not as "well" as you might think.

As someone who puts in the work, and who faces my feelings head-on whenever they arise, I find myself in the dark from time to time. And instead of running from the dark, I embrace it. I know that every time I allow myself to feel my feelings instead of running, I am becoming stronger and learning something about myself that will only add to my overall well-being as time goes on. I know that working through the darkness is what brings the light. Because once I've worked through something, I no longer need to hang onto it. I'm not walking around with it or thinking about it in the back of my head. I'm not wondering how I feel and feeling disconnected from myself and those around me. I'm not regretting *not* saying how I feel. I'm not upset with myself for not being honest about my truth. I'm not hiding. I'm thriving.

What I've found about peace is that it comes from living your life in accordance with your truth. It brings immense peace to know you're living in line with who you were meant to be. It's peaceful to be able to reflect on how much you've grown. It's peaceful to say how you truly feel. It's peaceful to know when to walk away. It's peaceful to know that you've put your best foot forward and done all that you could. It's peaceful to accept yourself. All of yourself. The light. The dark. You.

You might think you're happy and at peace, but maybe the truth is that you could be even *happier and more at peace*. And maybe you're not allowing yourself to face that truth because it's not comfortable or because you're unaware. It's time to stop sleeping on yourself. You're not here to be a floating ship, riding on the tide of others. That's not true peace. It's avoidance and detachment. It's a chronic fear of life itself. Peace is the expansive experience of both light and dark. You will never be at peace by tuning things out. You will just make your world increasingly small while you bottle up and suppress your rage. So, ask yourself honestly: are you sleepwalking or are you woke? Are you actually at peace or just telling yourself you are? And for those who are choosing to wake up, rise and shine, baby. True joy is waiting for you!

She pulled them out one by one
Little trinkets from her throat
A thread of thoughts that were buried
Under a layer of fog. She cleared it.
Those words, they were cutting
Pricking her insides
Deafening her ears
Swimming upwards
Fighting to be released
For years she waged the war
Weapon constantly in hand
Whenever triggered, she tensed harder
Around each syllable
Holding her breath for fear that they'd
Pour out unannounced
This was until the day she could no longer
Ignore them
Then it happened
They were triggered and out they fled
One by one the trinkets found
The light and caressed the world
With their meaning
Marking their surroundings
With permanent ink
And at once, she let out
Her breath
And sank into her truth.

The Truth Teller

CHAPTER 25

THE TRUTH TELLER

"Your truth will bring out the worst in others. Your love will tingle what they've numbed. Your authenticity will provoke closed minds. Your gratitude will irritate trolls. Your success will attract haters. Your empowerment will create enemies. Your uniqueness will antagonize fear. Your courage will attract cowards. Your sexuality will freak people out. Your joy will tug at their trauma. Your compassion will unmask envy. And love, that's what it's meant to do. Your aliveness will reveal many mental prisons, but help to set even more minds free."
— Tanya Markul (@tanyamarkul)

Let me start here with the understatement of the century: being a truth teller in our world today is challenging. If telling the truth were any easy feat, we'd all be doing it. We'd live in a world where people-pleasing wasn't such a common motivator for people. We'd have a society where people spoke their minds and didn't leave you on "read" or second-guessing interactions. You'd see people living as their full, embodied selves and not holding back for fear of how others may perceive them. Or for fear of how they will view themselves if they really take accountability and do that inner work. But obviously, this is not the world we currently inhabit.

In today's world, you often encounter lies, deception, passive-aggressiveness, manipulation, and surface-level interactions. You're faced with face-tune and highlight reels and contradictory messages and unsolicited opinions. And the sooner we can get real about this, both individually and collectively, the sooner we will be able to deal with the plethora of issues we are faced with in our world today. The first step is always awareness. We need to be aware that there are things we need to attend to within ourselves so that we can have the faith that we're moving in the direction meant for us.

It's the waking up to yourself, and subsequently, to others, that brings the clarity you seek.

So, let's start by dropping these figurative masks and beginning to embody ourselves. You're not going to become an integrated individual if your identity is fragmented. Or if you're hiding parts of yourself for survival. We need to unmask ourselves and allow our true essence to enter the equation to have any chance at a life of wholeness and freedom. We need to stop skimming the surface. We need to stop blindly following the crowd. They obviously don't know where they are going.

The crowd is just noise. It's what's popular in the moment, but ultimately, it doesn't serve a greater purpose. Your personal truth doesn't live in it. People follow the crowd for all sorts of reasons. They feel lost and they need something to believe in. They feel weak and need support from their fellow humans. They don't have the courage to stand alone. The truth is that the people who follow the crowd often don't even buy into what it is they are following. But they don't know another way. The other way is this: it's embodying your inner truth. It's being someone who is able and *willing* to stand tall in your truth and to express that truth to the world. It's being someone who doesn't just "go with the flow," but one who creates your own.

It's being brave enough to be honest, open and truthful about who you are. It's about waking up to ourselves.

I've always been a truth teller. No matter what the repercussions have ever been, I've never not said how I felt or stood up for what I believed in. And yes, I am remarkably proud of this (as anyone should be if they do the same). Because it *ain't easy*, that's for sure. You will certainly piss some people off. But the people who you will piss off are those whose life motto is "kindness is cool" or "go with the flow" or "be positive." (And how well are these people doing in life? I'll let you answer that one.) Telling the truth isn't what will get you the most friends. Because when people hear you telling the truth, they often get intimidated automatically. They know that as someone who is a truth teller, you're not going to beat around the bush. You're not here to play it safe. You're going to say things that might hurt. That might make people really uncomfortable. The truth can make people uncomfortable, but only those who run from it. So yes, telling the truth will piss some people off—but those just might not be your people. The *right* people will always stick around for your truth.

What you might not know about being a truth teller is how drastically your life will open up to you once you do so. You're not going to be doing things out of obligation. You'll have an easy time making decisions because you know your values and aren't going to compromise them. Your relationships will strengthen, because those who stick around for the truth are those willing to go to the depths of the earth with you. They'll be ride or dies, and you won't ever have to question your relationship with them because you know they love you for you, in full. You will have the freedom to say exactly what you want to say instead of holding back or hiding parts of yourself for survival. And for every person you piss off, you'll have a hand-ful of people who will feel inspired by you and feel safe enough to be their full selves in your presence. And what's more mean-ingful than that?

When you become an embodied individual, living in align-ment with your truth, you can wholeheartedly say that you know who you are and you love yourself for exactly that per-son. You can rest assured that you are living in line with your purpose, and you can be at peace with that. You will give to oth-ers out of the goodness of your heart and soul, not because you are "giving to get" or some other manipulative tactic. You come from a place of genuineness. You don't hold secrets. You don't store anger and other unwanted and suppressed emotions in your body. You speak your truth and feel your feelings and thus have a healthy outlet for them. You are free to be you with ev-ery single person in your life. When people ask you how you feel, you will know. You can relax into yourself. You can breathe easy. You can find true peace.

Throughout my journey I've gained an enormous amount of support and love from all parts of the world—both person-ally and professionally. But more than that, I'm free to be me and only me. And I've given myself *permission* to be me. I'm not living out of fear. I'm not looking externally for answers I can find within. I'm not mincing my words to make others com-fortable. I'm not living with a mask on. I'm able to be me, and only me, in any and every context of my life. I am proud of who I am and what I bring to the table in any situation. I don't dull myself down or hide myself for anyone. And it's because of this that I've been able to honor my purpose and encourage others to live out their truth as well. In other words, I've made an im-pact. I've inspired. My life has meaning because *I've* given it meaning instead of allowing others to color my life with *their* meaning.

The truth isn't meant to please everyone. But life's not about pleasing everyone, either. It's about living out our purpose. It's about loving and being loved for *who we actually are*, not who we are pretending to be. And we can't be loved for who we actually are if we're being something else. We can't people-please our way through life while simultaneously pleasing ourselves. We can't pretend to be more "positive" and still feel all our very valid human emotions. We can't live our lives authentically if we walk around clothed in our figurative masks. We need to get back to the basics: we need to get back to the truth.

To get to your truth, you're going to choose to wake up. You're going to tune out to tune in. You're going to build your foundation, piece by piece. You're going to do that inner work. You're going to face your fears and sit with yourself in the silence that you desperately need in order to hear your own self think and feel. You'll need to give other people back their projections. You'll need to set boundaries with people who you've grown apart from and who are infringing on your personal growth. You'll need to find your own flow instead of following that of someone else. You'll need to make the choice to embody yourself fully. You'll need to give yourself *permission* to do so. And that is how you will begin to build the confidence and self-love you need to live a life that makes you genuinely fulfilled and at peace. And that is how you will live authentically.

I'll never stop telling the truth, because I can't, anyway. Once you start becoming a truth teller, you're not going to be able to shut it off very easily. And it's for the best, truthfully. We shouldn't be making room for lies or false pretenses of any kind. Our world has enough of that already. But we don't have enough truth tellers. And in our world today, we desperately need more truth. We urgently need more embodied individuals who will lead the way and inspire others to be honest and authentic themselves. We need to create space for and welcome those in our lives to show up as themselves, not who we want them to be. We need less masks and more bare faces. We need more honesty. More transparency. More truth.

You know you've stepped into your truth when you can genuinely trust yourself. When you use your voice. When you have the courage to go your own way. When you have a solid foundation, including your own set of values, that you live by. When you don't restrict yourself to accommodate others at the expense of yourself. When you're able to set proper boundaries. When you're confident in who you are. When you honor your personal growth. There's a truth teller that lives within you. Go ahead and find it.

We all want to feel the freedom to be who it is that we were meant to be. And, after reading this book, I hope that you have a better understanding of what it entails to live an authentic life that truly means something to you. I hope you decide to do that inner work. I hope you find the courage to stand up for what you believe in and to use your voice. I hope you grant yourself the permission to live boldly and with intent. I hope you enable yourself to take off that figurative mask you've been hiding behind so that you can come back to your truth and meet it head on. The truth is the beginning, middle, and end of every story.

Truth be told, you should be running towards your inner truth as if your life depends on it. Because it does. And that's the ultimate truth.

ACKNOWLEDGMENTS

The truth is that, while I wrote every word of this book entirely on my own, I have several people to thank for being an integral part of my inspiration, motivation, and for challenging me in all of the best, most necessary ways. First, to my husband, Matt. Matt has been my biggest source of motivation as I wrote this book. He encouraged me to write on the days where I didn't think I had it in me to even make it to my desk. He listened patiently and passionately to every single iteration of the book. Matt has been my number one fan and loyal supporter throughout the process of building That Trendy Therapist™ and I cannot begin to thank him enough for that. Matt, you are the rock to my star. I couldn't and wouldn't have done it without you. Thank you for truly seeing me and for loving me unconditionally.

To my absolute best friend in the entire world, my mom. Muth, you are the reason that I am a truth teller. You have shown me, by example, the importance of being true to yourself and of making your voice heard. You were my best friend when I felt like I had none. You worked your ass off all my life, and continue to, and still never ever miss a beat. You are my inspiration to be a bold, bad-ass woman who is taken seriously in a world where women are usually not. You have reminded me of my strength when I've needed it most. You've been my biggest cheerleader since day one. You have saved me any and every time I have needed saving in any capacity. You've loved me unconditionally through everything. You are my role model, emotional support, fierce protector, advocate, BFF, mentor, and mommy all in one. I would literally not be here if it wasn't for you. Words don't express how much I love you, and you know I have words for everything.

To my rad lad of a dad for your analogies and worldly perspective you have so graciously imparted to me. As a man who grew up in all parts of the world, you've deeply broadened my worldview and how I view humanity. Dad, thank you for spending hours upon hours with me on my creativity since I was a little girl. Through art, dancing, music, poetry, movies, writing, storytelling, singing, taking photos, cooking, traveling the world... there is no stone left unturned when it comes to the endless ways you've inspired me to express myself. Thank you for showing me the beauty of the world and for taking such joy in teaching me all it is that you know. I learn something new each time I am around you. Thank you for keeping me grounded, humble and open-minded to all that this life has to offer. Thank you for loving me unconditionally, for protecting me consistently, and showing me what a respectable, honorable, humble, grounded man looks like. Thank you for always answering the phone without fail and for consistently being there. Thank you for always encouraging me to keep it natural, both internally and externally. I love you more than you will ever know.

To my brother, Dylan. There is no one else I'd rather have as my one and only sibling. Thank you for always sticking by me and for challenging me in the best of ways. Dylan, it is one of my greatest joys to be your big sis. You've always encouraged me to be the very best version of myself. You have been with me through it all and have loved me unconditionally, even when times were tough. We've learned, laughed, cried, partied, chilled, danced, and everything in between. All my core memories are with you, and I wouldn't have it any other way. Thank you for asking me the tough questions. Thank you for always providing levity and for making me laugh when I need it most. Thank you bringing the group together, always. Thank you for being loyal and for always showing up and following through. I promise to always be the best role model I can be. Fun, see!? Me gusta la radio. Good luck bro/sis. The list goes on, and I can't wait to continue growing alongside you. I love you infinitely.

To Eileen. Thank you for being the best therapist I could ever ask for. For never abandoning me. For always reminding me of my specialness. For holding up that mirror when I needed it most. For seeing me through every chapter since I got home from college. For helping me to see into my blind spots. For challenging me. For encouraging me. For giving me the necessary perspective. For being someone I know that I can always, always rely on and who will always be there. For listening. For not judging. For being patient. For being truly kind. For cheering me on in all of my endeavors. Thank you for all you have taught me and continue to teach me. I quite literally would not be this version of myself without you.

To Camilla for taking a chance on me and giving me my first job as a therapist. For teaching me how to work with my clients, but also with a team. For shining light on some of those spots I would've rather kept in the shade. For inspiring me to show up as the best version of myself in my career. For being the first boss I ever had that I could trust was guiding me in the right direction. For helping me build connections. For encouraging me to step up to the plate when I needed to. For empowering me. For listening. For sticking by me. For believing in me. For challenging me. For inspiring me.

To my Trendsetters, who have showered me with support since I started my account, @thattrendytherapist. You all have warmed my heart continually as you share with me how my words have inspired you. Your love and encouragement have motivated me and kept me focused on my purpose. Thank you all for sticking by me and for showing up. Thank you for sharing with me your innermost thoughts. Thank you for allowing me to share my words with you. You are all beams of light and I hope that you never, ever forget how much you matter and how much you are seen.

And last, but certainly not least, to my dearest Bubbie, who left the physical world in peace on September 21st, 2022. Bubbie, this is for you. You are still my best friend, and as I wrote this book, I thought of you throughout. You were the original truth teller before my mother and me. You knew I was going to be a writer. I know that you're up there, smiling down on me, jumping up and down and screaming, "I told you so! I knew you were going to be an author!" Yes, you did, Bubbie. But more than that, you taught me to live boldly and in color. And that, I will continue to do. I love you with all of me, and then some. Ain't that the truth!

www.ingramcontent.com/pod-product-compliance
Lightning Source LLC
Chambersburg PA
CBHW060903120626
46553CB00001B/187